The Clark Lectures 1982

Poetry and Metamorphosis

Poetry and Metamorphosis

CHARLES TOMLINSON

Cambridge University Press

CAMBRIDGE

LONDON   NEW YORK   NEW ROCHELLE

MELBOURNE   SYDNEY

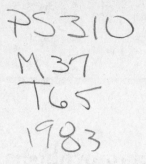

Published by the Press Syndicate of the University of Cambridge
The Pitt Building, Trumpington Street, Cambridge CB2 1RP
32 East 57th Street, New York, NY 10022, USA
296 Beaconsfield Parade, Middle Park, Melbourne 3206, Australia

First published 1983

Printed in Great Britain by Redwood Burn Ltd, Trowbridge, Wiltshire

Library of Congress catalogue card number: 82–19893

British Library cataloguing in publication data
Tomlinson, Charles
Poetry and metamorphosis.
1. Poetry – History and criticism
2. Metamorphosis in literature
I. Title
808.81'9337   PN1059.M53
ISBN 0 521 24848 5

RB

To Brenda

Contents

Acknowledgments

I owe grateful thanks to the Master and Fellows of Trinity College, Cambridge, for inviting me to give the Clark Lectures in the first place and for their hospitality to my wife and myself when I delivered them. The gracious kindness of the Master's wife, Lady Hodgkin, did much to make our stay in Cambridge a continuous pleasure.

I am chiefly indebted to my colleague Dr David Hopkins, with whom I had the opportunity to discuss some of my themes and whose interest and erudition gave me the courage to pursue my intuitive enquiries. I must also thank Professor William C. Dowling of the University of New Mexico for drawing my attention to Addison's fine poem *To Mr Dryden* quoted on page 10.

Note on the Texts

The principal quotations of poetry are from the following editions:

George Chapman, *Chapman's Homer, the Iliad, the Odyssey and the Lesser Homerica*, ed. Allardyce Nicholl, 2nd edn (Princeton University Press, 1967).

Abraham Cowley, *The Works,* 8th edn (1684).

John Dryden, 'The First Book of Homer's Ilias', *The Poems of John Dryden,* ed. James Kinsley (4 vols., Oxford University Press, 1958). Also in Garth's *Ovid* below.

T. S. Eliot, *Collected Poems 1909–1935* (Faber, London, 1936); *Four Quartets* (Faber, London, 1944); *The Waste Land, A Facsimile and Transcript* (Harcourt Brace Jovanovich, New York, 1971).

Ovid, *Ovids Metamorphoses, In Fifteen Books* (published by Sir Samuel Garth, MD, 1717).

Alexander Pope, *The Odyssey,* the Twickenham Edition of the Poems of Alexander Pope, ed. Maynard Mack (Methuen, London and Yale, New Haven, 1967).

Ezra Pound, *Three Cantos* (*Poetry,* June–August 1917); *Selected Poems* (Faber, London, 1948); *The Pisan Cantos* (Faber, London, 1949); *Seventy Cantos* (Faber, London,

1950), *The Spirit of Romance* (New Directions, New York, 1952); *Selection: Rock-Drill* (Faber, London, 1957); *Thrones* (New Directions, New York, 1959); *ABC of Reading* (Faber, London, 1961); *Drafts and Fragments* (New Directions, New York, 1968); *Collected Early Poems of Ezra Pound,* ed. Michael John King (New Directions, New York, 1976).

Prologue

Re-reading Ovid while editing *The Oxford Book of Verse in English Translation,* I found that the thought of metamorphosis and, indeed, of translation itself as being at once an act of metamorphosis and one of renewed creation entered ever more compellingly into one's mind. Metamorphosis, re-creation, translation – these and their meaning for poetry will be the theme of my four lectures.

In the first I shall be talking about a great translation of Ovid – not Golding's which Ezra Pound in *ABC of Reading* (p. 127) thought 'the most beautiful book in the language', but a later and, I think, wittier one.

My second and third lectures will go on to look at Ovid in metamorphosis – that is to say, they will try to see how two twentieth-century poets, Eliot and Pound, renovated the Ovidian spirit in their own work.

My final lecture, reaching back to my opening, will aim to show, in a short survey, how fundamentally translation and (re)-creation are allied, and how, when a writer is taken over by the voice of a former poet, the literary metempsychosis that results can equal and even surpass his own 'original' work.

1 An English Ovid

The theme I wish to open with is Ovid in translation. This will give me the opportunity to speak of that neglected classic, Sir Samuel Garth's composite edition of Ovid's *Metamorphoses* in English of 1717. Garth's edition represents the completion of a *Metamorphoses* begun in the 1690s during the business collaboration of the publisher Jacob Tonson and John Dryden. These two had recruited a team of (often young) translators for Ovid and other projects. This *Metamorphoses* was left unfinished at Dryden's death, after he himself had tackled many of the greatest parts of the poem. When I reach Ovid in metamorphosis you will, I hope, see how this grows out of and is intertwined with Ovid in translation.

Dryden seems to me the Poundian figure of his age, invigorating the talents of others – the young men he and Tonson had gathered round them – by his example and by his personal urging. Ovid seems to me a chief ancestor of literary modernism, and if the case of Joyce's *Ulysses* appears to deny that assertion, one can reply that Joyce's *Ulysses* is *The Odyssey* metamorphosed, and that Joyce, a directive influence on both Eliot and Pound, himself set forth on seas unknown emboldened by an epigraph concerning the artificer, Dedalus, from *The Metamorphoses,* Book VIII. We read on the title page of *Portrait of the Artist* 'Et ignotas animum dimittit in artes': 'And he abandoned his mind to obscure arts'. These obscure arts led Joyce to a point, some two decades later in *Finnegans Wake*, where opposites 'by the coincidance of their contraries reamalgamerge', and to the famous conclusion of Part I in which a couple of washer-women on the banks of the Liffey undergo Ovidian meta-morphosis into a stone and an elm. But this is to anticipate.

I take it that the wisdom of *The Metamorphoses* inheres in its imaginative vision of a world where all things are inter-related, where flesh and blood are near kin to soil and river, where man and animal share common instincts, where vege-tarianism is poetically the only defensible philosophy of life. This last point – quaint, as one might think it in the abstract – draws eloquence from Ovid and a comparable spread and sweep of the imaginative wing from Dryden in Book XV:

> While Kine to Pails distended Udders bring,
> And Bees their Honey redolent of Spring;
> While Earth not only can your Needs supply,
> But lavish of her Store, provides for Luxury,
> A guiltless Feast administers with Ease,
> And without Blood is prodigal to please [. . .]
> If Men with fleshy Morsels must be fed,
> And chaw with bloody Teeth the breathing Bread
> What else is this, but to devour our Guests,
> And barb'rously renew Cyclopean Feasts!

In this vision of the animals as 'our Guests', the speaker is Pythagoras, and there is a dramatic rightness in the way Ovid can allow him to rehearse the vegetarian argument, and later on the argument of metempsychosis (that hard word which in Joyce's *Ulysses* Molly Bloom asks Leopold Bloom the meaning of). For Ovid – and I imagine we have no evidence to show that he was either vegetarian or believed literally in metempsychosis – is using both arguments as a kind of imaginative wit, a 'dallying with surmise', to lead him to the climax at which his own voice and that of Pythagoras tally in a vision of cosmic unity, where, to quote Joyce, the 'coincidance' of 'contraries reamalgamerge', where time is

> Still moving, ever new: For former Things
> Are set aside, like abdicated Kings:

And every Moment alters what is done,
And innovates some Act, 'till then unknown.

And Dryden moves to one of the great climaxes of his version
of the poem with:

> All Things are alter'd, nothing is destroy'd,
> The shifted Scene for some new Show employ'd [. . .]
> Those very Elements, which we partake
> Alive, when dead some other Bodies make:
> Translated grow, have Sense, or can Discourse;
> But Death on deathless Substance has no Force.

The audacity, the *sprezzatura,* with which Dryden throws in
the word 'Translated' here – he who *translated* Chaucer into
modern English and who said he expected someone to do the
same for him one day – wittily incorporates the notion of
literary translation into the conception of an ongoing world
empowered by the metamorphosis of its own elements – mud
and stones into flesh and blood, flesh into trees, human into
divine. Dryden himself, it is not too much to say, metamorphosed – translated – elements from his own life into the
imaginative splendour of his English Ovid. Thus the political
Dryden – and it is a besetting sin of commentators to thrust
the political references to the forefront of an imagination
which digests political 'innovation' and 'act' to its own
purposes – the political Dryden brings to the realization of
Ovid in English (Ovid translated) the power of his own hard-
won wisdom, a wisdom then reaching, with Ovid, beyond
politics towards (one is tempted to say) the origin of species:

> The Face of Places, and their Form, decay;
> And that is solid Earth, that once was Sea:
> Seas in their Turn retreating from the Shore,
> Make solid Land, where Ocean was before;
> And far from Strands are Shells of Fishes found
> And rusty Anchors fix'd on Mountain-Ground.

Origin of species? If that is to exaggerate, perhaps one can
redeem the exaggeration by adding that Darwin, beginning
his career with works like *Structure and Disappearance of
Coral Reefs,* was to go on to write, in *On the Origin of*

Species, a book which dwells insistently and imaginatively on
the universal fact of metamorphosis.

In Ovid's universe, with its 'manifold variety', as one of his
editors has it, the metamorphoses come as reward, punishment, means of escape. Among the most beautiful are two
celebrations of married love – the change of the old couple
Baucis and Philemon into trees (Book VIII), so they shan't
experience separate deaths, and that of Ceyx and Alcyone
into sea-birds (Book XI). Alcyone, the daughter of Aeolus,
god of the winds, has tried to dissuade her husband, Ceyx,
from his sea-journey, and when her premonitions of his
drowning are fulfilled she, too, expresses the desire of Baucis
and Philemon – that of dying together:

> Happier for me, that all our Hours assign'd
> Together we had liv'd; ev'n not in Death disjoin'd!

She finds the drowned body of Ceyx, attempts to drown
herself and is metamorphosed:

> A Bird new-made, about the Banks she plies,
> Not far from Shore, and short Excursions tries;
> Nor seeks in Air her humble Flight to raise,
> Content to skim the Surface of the Seas [. . .]
> Now lighting where the bloodless Body lies,
> She with a Fun'ral Note renews her Cries:
> At all her Stretch, her little Wings she spread,
> And with her feather'd Arms embrac'd the Dead.

The translator again is Dryden, moving easily through
imaginative regions that Van Doren long ago said he was
incapable in – a measure of Dryden readily concurred with by
Eliot in his stress on the poet's lack of 'insight'. That
judgment still seems to be with us, a left-over from the era
when Dryden was convicted on insufficient evidence, of
contributing to a dissociation of sensibility that was never
more than a handy literary myth. Dryden – and the stories of
Deucalion and Pyrrha and of Baucis and Philemon are the
other supreme examples – as the poet of the tenderness and
pathos of married love! But, you will say, it took Ovid to
make him that. No doubt it did. Yet it would be no exaggeration to say of Dryden that, in writing about marriage, he

translated Ovid on to a higher plane. And Dryden proved capable, as no translator before or since, in providing the imaginative effort to find the exact tones for this delicate yet profound piece of wish-fulfilment in the Ceyx/Alcyone story:

> Then flick'ring to his pallid Lips, she strove
> To print a Kiss, the last Essay of Love.
> Whether the vital Touch reviv'd the Dead,
> Or that the moving Waters rais'd his Head
> To meet the Kiss, the Vulgar doubt alone;
> For sure a present Miracle was shown.
> The Gods their Shapes to Winter-Birds translate,
> But both obnoxious to their former Fate

– 'obnoxious to', namely 'exposed to', in that they are to live their new lives also as subject to the dangers of the sea. A moment later the element of wish-fulfilment is 'placed' by that sudden distancing, that playful and humane wit which, time and again and in the most unexpected places in Ovid, makes us re-adjust our expectations. We do not leave Ceyx and his wife, Alcyone, daughter of the god of the winds, on that note of pathos. There is a sort of divine mirth, a *hilaritas*, in the closing lines of their story of conjugal love:

> They bill, they tread; Alcyone compress'd,
> Sev'n Days sits brooding on her floating Nest:
> A wintry Queen: Her Sire at length is kind,
> Calms ev'ry Storm, and hushes ev'ry Wind;
> Prepares his Empire for his Daughter's Ease,
> And for his hatching Nephews smooths the Seas.

That distances, but does not destroy, both the terror and the pathos of this tale exposed to the sea of life. Now, the dream of dying together is one of the dreams that makes bearable a world of change from life to death. The gods are kind – sometimes – and commute death to metamorphosis, as here. And one sees the imaginative urgency that prompted but did not always give full force to those twelfth- and thirteenth-century versions of Ovid moralized in which metamorphosis is interpreted as being an earnest of the Christian doctrines of resurrection and immortality. The option of that interpretation is more tactfully left open by Golding's Elizabethan rendering:

> All things doo chaunge. But nothing sure doth perish

and in Dryden's

> All things are alter'd, nothing is destroy'd

and a few lines later in

> But Death on deathless Substance has no Force.

Dryden, and his collaborators in the Garth Ovid, in transmitting the wisdom of Ovid's great vision, transmit also the undertow of that worry which accompanies the wisdom and which declares itself and yet refuses to become a feast of luxury on itself, by means of that delicate wish-fulfilment which I have mentioned. Wish-fulfilment, fantasy, 'dallying with surmise' – I do not want to give the impression that *The Metamorphoses* offers a merely Nietzschean view of art, as the illusion which makes life tolerable. What is still being asked in many of the stories – particularly in those transformations into vegetable, mineral or stone – and asked often against the grain of the story, focuses on what it is like to become an object. Even in the act of consenting to this universe of fecund change, even in the act of consenting to become (say) a tree, an intimation, a *frisson* of real death touches the imagination. One senses, sometimes momentarily, sometimes at greater length, what Eliot speaks of on the occasion of Celia Coplestone's martyrdom in *The Cocktail Party,* the 'reluctance of the body to become a *thing'*.

Given the option between tree and stone I suppose you and I would choose to become trees, would we not? In the ninth of the *Duino Elegies,* as the sequence hovers between the sufferings, the *Klage*, of the previous elegies, and the desire to praise, Rilke introduces a contemplation of the laurel, laurel perhaps that grew in the precincts of Schloss Duino. In the Leishman–Spender version it goes:

> Why, when this span of life might be fleeted away
> as laurel, a little darker than all
> the surrounding green, with tiny waves on the border
> of every leaf (like the smile of a wind): oh, why
> *have* to be human [. . .]?

'Warum dann / Menschliches müssen [. . .]?' Daphne is
never named here, but, with a lovely implicitness, her transformation into laurel hovers over the fantasy that springs up
in this hesitation in the face of destiny. Wouldn't one sooner,
in certain circumstances, be a tree than human? And the
thought gathers to itself those mollifying 'tiny waves [. . .]
like the smile of a wind', and one remembers that in *The
Sonnets to Orpheus,* in a further metamorphosing of Ovid's
tale, Daphne, now changed to a laurel tree, is still animate
enough to wish for the metamorphosis of her pursuer into the
wind. As in Ovid, a tree is endowed with lingeringly human
feelings. Throughout *The Metamorphoses* people are also
changed into birds. That, conceivably, would be an even
better choice, if choice were a possibility in the matter, or
would we stick at laurels on the primitive impulse that trees
outlast birds? Springs, streams are perhaps more complicated
matters. Let's stay with the more manageable duality which
ends *Finnegans Wake* Part I, from Shem and Shaun to stem
and stone, the human voice losing its power to speak as it
merges sleepily with inanimate creation, as it becomes a
thing: 'My foos won't moos. I feel as old as yonder elm [. . .]
My ho head halls. I feel as heavy as yonder stone.'

Tree or stone? Rilke draws consciously from Ovid, choos-
ing the fluidity of tree and wind. Joyce refers back wittily to
The Metamorphoses with his two washerwomen transformed
into 'yonder elm' and 'yonder stone', and he is gaily detached
from the immersion he is evoking. Wordsworth, on the other
hand, surrenders himself to the fascination of the stoniness of
stone and even to the possibility of sharing in it. Here, he is
Ovid's antithesis, for this fantasy of petrification, as we shall
see presently, repelled Ovid himself. The protagonist of one
of Wallace Stevens' poems, *Le Monocle de Mon Oncle,* only
goes as far as wishing himself to be 'a *thinking* stone'. The old
beggar woman in Wordsworth's early play *The Borderers*
says: 'I'd rather be / A stone than what I am', but she speaks
under immeasurable duress. Lucy of the Lucy poems is
'Rolled round in earth's diurnal course, / With rocks and
stones and trees': there is a rightness in that, but it is the poet

who speaks on her behalf and not she. In a lesser known poem of Wordsworth's, from Sara Hutchinson's notebook, 'These chairs they have no words to utter', the poet protagonist, in a room where 'The ceiling and floor are as mute as a stone', indulges the dream that in this stone-bound stillness he can lie 'Happy as they who are dead'. However, the 'reluctance of the body to become a *thing*' forces this poet, for whom the word 'thing' was obsessive, back into the world of the sun, where

> The things which I see
> Are welcome to me.

By the end of the poem, he returns to wishing that life itself could be penetrated by this mute, as it were stone-enveloped 'quiet of death / Peace, peace, peace'. This longing for 'a repose which ever is the same', around which Wordsworth's mind circles still in a much later poem, *Ode to Duty*, elicits a swifter response from the imagination in the Lucy poem because she is not only in repose, but being 'rolled round', and also because 'rocks and stones' are tempered by the presence of 'trees', which is the rhyme word that clinches and concludes the poem, taking off from 'She neither hears nor sees' something of its full horror by calling on however momentary a response from that primitive impulse which makes us prefer to be a tree rather than a stone and which originally, no doubt, endowed trees with dryads:

> A slumber did my spirit seal;
>   I had no human fears:
> She seemed a thing that could not feel
>   The touch of earthly years.
>
> No motion has she now, no force;
>   She neither hears nor sees;
> Rolled round in earth's diurnal course,
>   With rocks and stones and trees.

Stem or stone? When Daphne, pursued by Apollo, undergoes her transformation into a laurel in Book I, the change is ultimately to be seen as beneficent. The body is willing to become a thing, but a thing which retains something of its

own nature. Like all profound change the incident is touched
with the pain of strangeness, the pain of initiation. But only
touched. Daphne's wished-for metamorphosis is swift, like
that in a speeded-up film of natural change:

> Gape Earth, and this unhappy Wretch intomb;
> Or change my Form, whence all my Sorrows come.
> Scarce had she finish'd, when her Feet she found
> Benumb'd with Cold, and fasten'd to the Ground:
> A filmy Rind about her Body grows;
> Her hair to Leaves, her arms extend to Boughs:
> The Nymph is all into a Laurel gone;
> The Smoothness of her Skin remains alone.
> Yet Phoebus loves her still, and casting round
> Her Bole, his Arms, some little Warmth he found.
> The Tree still panted in th'unfinish'd Part:
> Not wholly vegetive, and heav'd her Heart.
> He fixt his Lips upon the trembling Rind;
> It swerv'd aside, and his Embrace declin'd.

However, now the change is complete, Apollo declares

> because thou canst not be
> My Mistress, I espouse thee for my Tree,

and he goes on to explain that this laurel will be the Prize of
Honour and that it will crown 'The deathless Poet and the
Poem'. So Ovid, the deathless poet – and how winningly he
bestows the compliment on himself, and earns it in the act of
writing the deathless poem – can go on to speak on behalf of
Daphne as Wordsworth spoke on behalf of Lucy, and report
her reaction to Apollo's words:

> The grateful Tree was pleas'd with what he said;
> And shook the shady Honours of Her Head.

If Daphne's change is only *touched* with the pain of transformation, the arboreal change of the faithful old couple,
Baucis and Philemon, though beneficent like hers, is haunted
by an image of real death. In Dryden's version there are
differences from Ovid here, his imaginative grasp of the
meaning of marriage giving an added pathos to this tale. He
outdoes Ovid in a manner that makes the concluding couplet
of the following passage from Addison's *To Mr. Dryden* – a

poem that finely sees translation as a type of metamorphosis –
no mere hyperbole:

> O may'st thou still the Noble Tale prolong,
> Nor Age, nor Sickness interrupt thy Song:
> Then may we wondring read how Human Limbs,
> Have water'd Kingdoms, and dissolv'd in Streams [. . .]
> How some in Feathers, or a ragged Hide
> Have liv'd a second Life, and different Natures try'd.
> Then will thy *Ovid*, thus transform'd, reveal
> A Nobler Change than he himself can tell.
>
> (*Examen Poeticum,* 1693)

Dryden's *Baucis and Philemon* from Book VIII is one of
the great literary narratives. As translation, it certainly equals
his own best work. Indeed, one finds oneself asking whether
Dryden with a Shakespearian mastery of pace and tone, with
a glance at the Bible here, a hint of La Fontaine there, by a
deepening of the sense of the sacredness of married love, did
not surpass his great Latin original by a very wide margin
indeed. I cannot linger here on the couple's hospitality to the
gods who call as strangers, graced as the episode is with
unstinted details such as (of Baucis):

> With Leaves and Bark she feeds her Infant Fire

(lightly presaging the later change to trees in 'Leaves and
Bark', gently witty on 'Infant') or her kettle:

> Like burnish'd Gold the little seether shone

or the old couple's attempt (and here the tenderness
modulates into humour) at catching their goose as a sacrifice
to the gods:

> Her with malicious Zeal the Couple view'd;
> She ran for Life, and limping they pursu'd.

My own concern is with the moment of wished-for change.
Their continuing life is not like that continuing life of birds
known to Ceyx and Alcyone. Philemon has asked of the gods

> We beg one Hour of Death, that neither she
> With Widow's Tears may live to bury me,
> Nor weeping I, with wither'd Arms, may bear
> My breathless Baucis to the Sepulcher.

The gods grant this and they further commute the 'one Hour of Death' into metamorphosis – to an oak and a linden tree. Yet the image of a death it remains – much more so than Daphne's laurel, twisting away from Apollo and finally nodding its crest:

> New Roots their fasten'd Feet begin to bind,
> Their Bodies stiffen in a rising Rind:
> Then, ere the Bark above their Shoulders grew,
> They give, and take at once a last Adieu.
> At once, Farewell, O faithful Spouse, they said;
> At once th'incroaching Rinds their closing lips invade.

Neither the sound of that final line – the hard c's narrowing off the cavity of the throat as one speaks them – nor the line's sinister lengthening out into an alexandrine as the growth takes over, permits us to forget that this is a death stifling out the human voice. And this stifling out of the human voice, as the body becomes a thing, is a theme I shall return to shortly. Suffice it to say, 'th'incroaching Rinds' resemble less Daphne's 'filmy Rind' than another transformation – that of the nymph Perimele in Book VIII to the soil and rock of an island. Here, we realize how close pulsation can come to petrification. The speaker is Achelous the river god, who is pursuing her:

> The Nymph still swam, tho' with the Fright distrest,
> I felt her Heart leap trembling in her Breast;
> But hard'ning soon, whilst I her Pulse explore,
> A crusting Earth cas'd her stiff Body o'er.

Stem or stone? The one veritable epic of petrification takes place in Book V of *The Metamorphoses* after Perseus has freed Andromeda from the sea-monster and has claimed her as his bride. These petrifications, which he brings about by brandishing the Gorgon's head at his enemies, are punishments of those who would like to prevent his marriage with the bride he has justly obtained. If one's mind balks at imagining unpleasant things as happening to oneself, the difficulty is eased by contriving a situation in which they happen to others – and to others who have deserved them. Justice, as I have said, is on Perseus' side. The imagining of these petrifications arises from such a vivid sense of the 'reluctance of the body to become a *thing*' that imagination triumphs over justice, while at the same time getting some of its gusto from the fact that justice is being done. Also, the petrification immediately threatens to stifle back human utterance into the inanimate: 'My foos won't moos [. . .] My ho head halls', 'These chairs they have no words to utter.' Neither does a tongue that has just turned into marble:

> While yet he spoke, the dying Accents hung
> In Sounds imperfect on his Marble Tongue;
> Tho' chang'd to Stone, his Lips he seem'd to stretch
> And thro' th'insensate Rock wou'd force a speech.

This is the end of Nileus

> who vainly said he ow'd
> His origin to Nile's prolifick Flood

– from water to marble, one of many like changes:

> Their safety in their Flight Two Hundred found,
> Two Hundred by Medusa's Head were ston'd.

The palace of King Cepheus, father of Andromeda, becomes virtually a massive cemetery cluttered with men who have turned into their own funerary monuments. They are all there to aid Phineus, who had formerly been promised Andromeda but who made no attempt to rescue her from the sea-monster. He is cowardly, and when he sees the fate of his friends, he begs Perseus for his life. Perseus 'stones' him, too. And poor Phineus is not merely turned to stone. His stone image, the fact of his death, embodies what essentially his life was – that of a coward – and, self-judged, thus he stands:

> As here and there he strove to turn aside,
> The Wonder wrought, the Man was petrify'd:
> All Marble was his Frame, his humid Eyes
> Dropp'd Tears, which hung upon the Stone like Ice.
> In suppliant Posture, with uplifted Hands,
> And fearful Look, the guilty Statue stands.

Images like this strike deep – beyond any mere sense of justice done – into the mind of a reader, and bring home with far greater finality than arboreal change the knowledge that our death sets the seal on all that we are, that such choices as we have made are now irrevocable, that death has made an object of our past weaknesses since nothing can now redeem or uncongeal them.

In the episode of Perseus and his assailants, Dryden has gone off duty in the Garth edition. The translator is one Arthur Maynwaring and very fine he is, like many of the secondary hands in this great version – young Mr Pope, Congreve, Gay, Mr Vernon who did the episode of the nymph turning into an island, Addison whose appearances are always to be watched for, and whose story of Phaeton and the chariot of the sun in Book II possesses such narrative power, that one cannot but wonder what sort of rôle Dryden played in the final draft. Perhaps one day, someone with a preternaturally fine ear or some energetic young scholar will solve this question in a number of these versions, encouraged by the existence in the William Andrews Clark Memorial Library of George Stepney's manuscript of his version of Juvenal's '8th Satire'.[1] That same version of Stepney's, as it appeared in Dryden's edition of Juvenal, was radically and forcefully revised. By Dryden himself? A note on the Stepney manuscript, reputedly in Pope's handwriting, believes that to be the case, and adds: 'This was what that great Man did for almost all his acquaintance.' I merely touch on the existence of this Poundian characteristic of Dryden's, prompted by wondering if Maynwaring's handling of the Perseus episode could be all his own work. It is certainly stamped with a bold use of enjambement which isn't entirely Drydenesque. But that way lies further divagation.

I began my samples of Maynwaring with, you will recall, the episode of Nileus being turned to stone, and

> the dying Accents hung
> In Sounds imperfect on his Marble Tongue.

I was using that as an example of the way the fact of metamorphosis, and the acquiescence in a world based on

---

1 See George Stepney's *Translation of the 8th Satire of Juvenal*, ed. T. and E. Swedenberg (University of California Press, Berkeley and Los Angeles, 1948).

metamorphosis, is so often haunted by a nakedly human imagining of what death is like, and by the 'reluctance of the body to become a *thing*'. The involvement of tongue with word, and the tongue's capacity or incapacity to utter human sounds, would appear to be a theme close to a poet's most intimate sense of himself, whether he stutters it out like Hopkins in *The Wreck of the Deutschland* – 'where, where was a, where was a place?' – and later has to wrap his tongue around that 'lush-kept, plush-capped sloe' and mouth it until he can force out heart's truth 'past telling of tongue', or whether, like Ovid, he runs the theme through a gamut of fables. That marble tongue of Nileus comes, in fact, at the dead end of a gamut which, in its upper reaches, explores that other concern of Ovid's – the frontier between human and animal, the mixture of humanity and animality in sexual adventure and violence, the question of how far the truly human can still inhere in the irrational and instinctual. Like the exploration of death – and Orpheus, venturer into Hades, is, one reminds oneself, Ovid's ideal poet as he is Rilke's – this exploration of the gamut between human and animal releases a characteristic *frisson,* often at the moment of metamorphosis – at the moment when human language, of which the poet is the supreme articulator, is becoming impossible, where meanings are literally 'past telling of tongue'.

In story after story, as the poet sings on, human voices plunge or falter into animality, wishfully, or sometimes because their human nature – and here one feels the Dantescan element in Ovid – has been taken over by a sub-human trait of character. Thus Lycaon (Book I) is, so to speak, 'damned' for his inhumanity by Jove, and turned into a wolf:

> Howling he fled, and fain he would have spoke;
> But human Voice his brutal Tongue forsook.

This same drama of utterance is recurrent throughout *The Metamorphoses*. Io (Book I), in a story of Jove's amours, which treads a mysterious, characteristically Ovidian frontier between the comic and the painful, is changed to a beautiful heifer:

> She strove to speak, she spoke not, but she low'd:
> Affrighted with the noise, she look'd around,
> And seem'd t'inquire the Author of the Sound.

She happens upon her father, the river god Inachus

> And lick'd his palms, and cast a piteous Look;
> And in the Language of her Eyes, she spoke.
> She wou'd have told her Name, and ask'd Relief,
> But wanting Words, in Tears she tells her Grief
> Which, with her Foot she makes him understand;
> And prints the name of *Io* in the Sand.

Inachus, who has been searching for her, realizes he has found his daughter:

> So found, is worse than lost: with mutual Words
> Thou answer'st not, No Voice thy Tongue affords
> But Sighs are deeply drawn from out thy Breast;
> And Speech deny'd, by Lowing is expressed.
> Unknowing, I prepar'd thy Bridal Bed

and he launches off into his complaint, as into an aria begun with a slight modulation of a repeated phrase – the modulation being that rhyme of 'Lowing / Unknowing' with which Dryden so expertly and so simply gathers up the echo into the now to be unfolded lament. This story, unlike that of Lycaon, ends benignly with the return from heifer to woman:

> She tries her Tongue; her Silence softly breaks,
> And fears her former Lowings when she speaks.

And Dryden, here, uses the resources of English to make a little more explicit that drama of utterance which is in the Latin, yet not in the words in the same way:

> She tries her Tongue; her Silence softly breaks,

The second half of this line can be read transitively – she breaks her silence – or intransitively – silence yields itself up as she regains intelligible speech. Once more, it's the simplicity of the effect that reinforces the accuracy of the perception: she breaks her own silence by 'trying her tongue', then – and the mid-line pause registers the anxiety (ours and hers) as to whether she'll actually speak – she both breaks her silence and hears it break:

> She tries her Tongue; her Silence softly breaks,

and, indeed, not until the close of the ensuing line is the anxiety resolved by rhyme – or rather wittily half-resolved:

> And fears her former Lowings when she speaks.

A darker episode than that of Io, and another variation on our theme, is to be found in one of Addison's splendid contributions to our English Ovid, the tale of Echo. She is cursed by Juno with a grotesque speech impediment:

> for though her voice was left
> Juno a curse did on her Tongue impose
> To sport with every Sentence in the Close.

She falls in love with Narcissus – the part of Ovid's episode that deals with him, incidentally, seems to have penetrated deeply the long, cancelled passage on Saint Narcissus in Eliot's *The Waste Land*. Finally Narcissus, hopelessly in love with his own reflection, dies and

> To the cold Shades his flitting Ghost retires,
> And in the Stygian Waves itself admires.

But before this, Echo finds her supreme fulfilment in fitting her tongue to the voice of this man she loves, but who loves himself, and she utters on her own behalf the self-involved laments he directs at his reflection:

> She answer'd sadly to the Lover's Moan,
> Sigh'd back his Sighs and groan'd to ev'ry Groan.

Ovid's *Metamorphoses* take us through the whole scale of moans and groans, sighings, lowings, howlings, hissings, apesounds, croakings, whinnyings, bat-talk, bear-roaring, to the voicelessness of fishes. My own conclusion comes with the voicelessness – the loss of tongue – that dominates that story of the sexual violence of Tereus and 'The change of Philomel, by the barbarous king / So rudely forced', in words from T. S. Eliot's *The Waste Land*. In Garth's Ovid (Book VI) the story is told by Mr Croxall. He's not the best translator in the world for this haunting tale, and there are one or two weak lines. All the same, the general run of the thing has energy, and moments occur when this minor writer takes fire and excels himself.

One hears nothing from Ovid about Philomela's 'inviolable voice' – Eliot's phrase – when she has become a nightingale. But one sees what it was in this tale about eloquence and also about not having a voice that drew Eliot – the poet for whom 'voices', 'words', 'silence' all vibrate meaningfully, though with meanings that threaten to elude the speaker. For an early protagonist like Prufrock, 'It is impossible to say just what I mean!' Gerontion hears the silence of 'The word within a word, unable to speak a word, / Swaddled with darkness'. 'I gotta use words when I talk to you', says Sweeney in Eliot's most original dramatic work. 'What words have we? / I should like to be in a crowd of beaks without words' runs one of the desperate cancellations from *The Waste Land* manuscript. Beaks without words – this is where we are at the end of Philomela's tale, with Philomela and Procne metamorphosed into birds of blood-spattered plumage, and Tereus with the most dangerous beak of the three:

> Fix'd on his Head the crested Plumes appear.
> Long is his Beak, and sharpen'd like a Spear.

Any summary of the tale makes it sound merely ghastly. Here is mine: Tereus goes to Athens to fetch Philomela to visit her sister Procne (his wife) in Thrace. Already in Athens he is beginning to lust after Philomela. On the way back he rapes her, cuts out her tongue and imprisons her in a hunting lodge. When the truth of the matter gets to Procne, she frees Philomela and then cannibalizes Tereus' son Itys, serving him up to his father, after which Philomela appears drenched in gore and hurls Itys' severed head at him. This comes at a point when the two women have worked themselves up to a pitch of hysteria. Tereus is also a hysteric – earlier in the poem he succeeds in making himself cry at his own rhetoric where he's persuading Philomela's father how badly Procne wants to see her sister. The hurling of the severed head marks a climax of hysteria in a poem which itself refuses to be hysterical. With the hurling of the head, the attitude is not that of (say) Richard Strauss's opera *Salome,* where we are being solicited into palpitating vicariousness, where we are being asked whether we, too, wouldn't perhaps like a taste of that other severed head – John the Baptist's – Salome is busy kissing. The firm Dantescan power of Ovid lies in the way he portrays the ever-accelerating, self-injuring, self-damning impetus of this gang of hysterics – 'gang' is the word Croxall uses to describe the crowd of Bacchantes that Procne takes to free Philomela, Procne herself having donned the pelt of a stag as well as a garland of vine leaves

> And with religious Yellings [filled] the Skies.

What Ovid did with this tale – and his doings compelled Eliot's imagination to make of it an objective correlative to his own wholly interior drama – was to evolve the vortex of hysterias out of his own sense of the way we unpack our hearts with words, allowing them to intensify and doubly corrupt feelings that are already suspect. A poet might well have gone for the hysteria alone. Shakespeare, or whoever wrote *Titus Andronicus,* luxuriates in a debased recollection of Philomela's cut-out tongue in the melodrama of Lavinia's even gorier mutilations in that play. In Ovid this theme of the tongue always keeps in sight the theme of words, in a kind of extended piece of wit-writing, though this is wit-writing that is never *merely* witty, but capable of the most telling of tragic ironies.

We may end among 'beaks without words', but the vortex of hysterias begins with a plethora of words – with Tereus' speech of persuasion to Philomela's father:

> The Eloquence of Love his Tongue inspires
> And, in his Wife's, he speaks his own Desires;
> Hence all his Importunities arise,
> And Tears unmanly trickle from his Eyes.

He is just as eloquent when, after the rape, he lies to his wife

about her sister being dead, and his eloquence succeeds once
more in squeezing out those pathic tears – Ovid's handling of
the story is remarkable for the way, early on, one is made to
feel words breeding on words their own insincerities. The
trouble with Philomela is that she, too, talks too much – uses
too many words for her own good. After the rape, she vividly
and at length evokes for Tereus just what morally he has
done. It's a speech of over thirty lines in Croxall's version,
and, like Tereus' own efforts, only too successful as a
rhetorical performance with all the stops out: it so tells on the
imagination of Tereus that he's flung unresisting into his
hysteric's vision of rapidly alternating contraries, and two
couplets here very ably catch the lurching unpredictability of
his behaviour:

> Struck with these Words, the Tyrant's guilty Breast
> With Fear, and Anger, was, by turns, possest;
> Now, with Remorse his Conscience deeply stung,
> He drew the Falchion that beside him hung,
> And [. . .]

He doesn't, however, impale himself because of that 'Con-
science deeply stung'. He doesn't cut her throat, as she asks
him, to get rid of the stain on her character. 'Struck with
these Words', what he wants is their source – the tongue that
made him hear what he's done and which threatens to tell
'the pitying Rocks' if she can't get free. The severed tongue –
and this is the bit that pleased 'those damned Elizabethans' as
Matthew Arnold called them – continues

> Murmuring with a faint imperfect Sound:
> And, as a Serpent writhes his wounded Train,
> Uneasy, panting, and possess'd with Pain.

When Philomela gets the truth of the matter to Procne by
weaving the words she can't speak into a piece of tapestry,
Croxall reiterates the tongue theme that he has seen at work
in Ovid: Procne reads the tapestry and

> In such tumultuous Haste her Passions sprung,
> They chok'd her Voice, and quite disarm'd her Tongue.
> No room for female Tears; the Furies rise,
> Darting vindictive glances from her eyes.

English usage here results in the repetition of 'tongue'.
Golding's version of 1567 has a similar turn of phrase: 'But
sorrow tied hir tongue.' This is all rather more concrete than
the Latin which simply says 'grief choked her utterance'. But
if the English over-insists, the insistence is not merely fanci-
ful, and its concreteness is perfectly in tune with Ovid's
subsequent tragic wit as it shifts from tongue to words, from
words to silence.

The last three reiterations of the motif of the tongue in
Croxall's version are all derived straight from the Latin.
Procne, having got her sister back, works on her and on her-
self to dream up the right kind of punishment for Tereus.
Seeing that Philomela can only speak with her hands, 'In
Procne's breast the rising Passions boil', and, as they boil
over, she rushes from the idea of setting the palace on fire to

> Or, his false Tongue with racking Engines seize;
> Or, cut away the Part that injur'd you.

(This isn't quite some Freudian identification of tongue and
penis, but it darts back accurately, even while charting
Procne's mounting hysteria, to the manner in which, as we've
noted, Tereus' sexual feelings feed his eloquence.)

> A while, thus wav'ring, stood the furious Dame,
> When Itys fondling to his Mother came.

The artistically gripping thing about what I have called the
poem's vortex of hysterias is that there are sudden lulls,
moments when we feel the poet's own control in the manner
in which he spaces out the eruptions of feeling, moments
when, for all that, the lulls are terrible for the brooding they
imply. The child Itys could hardly have appeared at a worse
time. Procne, as one expects, sees the father in the son, and
starts

> Forming the direful Purpose in her head

– of sacrificing him, that is. But as he approaches

> And he accosts her in a prattling tone
> Then her tempestuous Anger was allay'd,
> And in its full Career her vengeance stay'd.

What leads to the child's undoing is this obsessive theme of
The Metamorphoses that we've been exploring, exemplified in
the fact that he *can* prattle. She turns from prattling child to
silent sister:

> While this fond Boy (she said) can thus express
> The moving Accents of his fond Address;
> Why stands my sister of her Tongue bereft

and from now on, there is no holding back on cutting the
child to pieces, or on the hysteric involvement of Philomela
too – she who begins to relish the situation as she evidently
relished the dressing down she gave Tereus before he
silenced her.

Ovid thoroughly understands (to borrow the terms of a
later culture) the psychology of damnation, yet in the very act
of dramatizing it he can distance the insane hysteria of his
protagonists, as in the black humour of the final appearance
of the tongue theme. Philomela flings the head of Itys at
Tereus:

> Nor ever long'd so much to use her Tongue
> And with a just Reproach to vindicate her Wrong.

The tale as a whole works through a clear sense of how
hysteria involves its victims in a train of subhuman feeling
and subhuman action, and how it thrives on a diet that
combines the irrational and the calculating. Beginning in lust,
the story ends in wrath. The sheer animal violence, right up
to the close when Tereus seizes his sabre to despatch the
sisters, rather than the culminating metamorphosis into
birds, is what engages Ovid's imaginings. We only know from
legend what sort of birds the sisters became and there is no
question in Ovid of the nightingale bursting into song. In all
this Ovid brings fully to mind Dante's own sense of the
sullen, the violent, the wrathful, of those who must suffer the
untying of the knot of anger – 'e d'iracondia van solvendo il
nodo'. This awareness of what people do to themselves, of
the nature of self-destruction and the tortures of the self-
enclosed ego, unexpectedly unites the poet of *The Metamorphoses* and the poet of *The Divine Comedy*, nowhere more so

– and this must be my final example – than when Erisichthon
(Book VII), having wilfully and persistently flouted the
goddess Ceres, is visited with unappeasable hunger by
Famine herself, and ends by devouring his own flesh:

> He grows more empty, as the more supply'd,
> And endless Cramming but extends the Void [. . .]
> Now Riches hoarded by Paternal Care
> Were sunk, the Glutton swallowing up the Heir [. . .]
> At last all Means, as all Provisions, fail'd;
> For the Disease by Remedies prevail'd;
> His Muscles with a furious Bite he tore,
> Gorg'd his own tatter'd Flesh, and gulphed his Gore.
> Wounds were his Feast, his Life to Life a Prey,
> Supporting Nature by its own Decay.

(Mr Vernon)

Of the 'quattro grand'ombre', the four great shades who come
forward to greet Dante in *Inferno* IV, Ovid is third in line
after Homer and Horace – the fourth is Lucan. As Ezra
Pound has it in his essay on Arnaut Daniel: 'Dante has
learned also of Ovid [. . .] although he talks so much of
Virgil.'

I've tried, so far, to present some aspects of the Ovidian
vision as it is brought over in a major English translation –
one that ought to be part of our literary heritage, as Pope's
Homer once was. I shall next look at Ovid in metamorphosis,
at the Dantescan Ovid who influenced Eliot and at how he
has been transformed and renewed in twentieth-century
poetry. This also provides an examplar of the wisdom of *The
Metamorphoses* – in Dryden's words in Book XV:

> Nor dies the Spirit, but new Life repeats
> In other Forms, and only changes Seats.

2   T. S. Eliot: Meaning and Metamorphosis

In *The Metamorphoses* the story of Tereus, Philomela and the severed tongue comes as a climax to several other tales, where the drama depends on the poet's sense of having a tongue, or of feeling it turn to marble, or of hearing it lapse out into bird or beast noises or into silence. The possession of a tongue and our capacity to use it, 'the involvement of tongue with word [as I have said] would appear to be a theme close to the poet's most intimate sense of himself'. This is an awareness that draws T. S. Eliot magnetically to the Tereus–Philomela story in writing *The Waste Land*. Long before that, to be tongue-tied, to be incapable of saying just what one means, already haunted Eliot's poetry. At times he even yearns for tonguelessness, or his protagonists do. Other poets – Hopkins with his 'where, where was a, where was a place?', the Peruvian Vallejo with his 'Desde ttttales códigos' ('According tttto such codes') – other poets have *forced* the impeded tongue into speech.[1] Hopkins even forces it into a tormented lyricism. But Eliot disdains what would perhaps have seemed to him such expressionist self-advertisement. More impersonally, he does however choose a fragmented art form where psychic wholeness can yet be hinted at by the use of myth and of metamorphosis.

---

1   See César Vallejo, *Poemas Humanos, a bilingual edition* (Grove Press, New York, 1968), p. 26.

'I am no longer concerned with metaphors but with meta-morphoses.' Thus Georges Braque in *Cahiers D'Art*. His words might stand as epigraph not only to the modernist phase in painting, fragmenting reality to reconstitute it in non-imitative forms, but also to certain aspects of the collage-poems of Pound and Eliot. Literature will go on to concern itself with metaphors, of course, though what Braque seems to mean by metaphor in painting is that by realistically imitating the appearance of an object, by letting your imitation stand in place of that object, you are denying the creative mind its full plastic power. By metamorphosis, as distinct from metaphor in Braque's sense, the mind could transform that object into a less predictable, a more variously faceted image. Music, which does not concern itself with metaphor in any exact sense of the meaning, also, in the hands of Schoenberg, followed the way of fragmentation, building new wholes out of its atonalized constituents, venturing on new sound paths. In both visual and literary art, the notions of fragmentation and metamorphosis travel together, as at the climax of *The Waste Land* within sight of Babel:

> *Poi s'ascose nel foco che gli affina*
> *Quando fiam uti chelidon* – O swallow swallow
> *Le Prince d'Aquitaine à la tour abolie*
> These fragments I have shored against my ruins
> Why then Ile fit you. Hieronymo's mad againe.
> Datta. Dayadhvam. Damyata.
>   Shantih shantih shantih

Do we *hear* that any longer, or have we lost the Babelic din it makes to the rumble of a thousand commentaries? Five languages, and their differing metrical forms – or bits of them. Read aloud like this, without warning, the famous climax recalls, perhaps, our forgotten first reading, as the mind re-adjusts itself to take in and differentiate all that sheer noise, and attempts to reconstitute noise as meaning. In the reconstituting, we help to complete a metamorphosis. Literary art was always like this – to *some* degree; so that what we are reading *now* reshapes what we have read up to this point. But Eliot foreshortens the process, speeds it up, involves you in the crisis of it, and the languages are a part of that. From our first reading, scarcely possible to recall, perhaps what still remains in the memory is a sense of pleasant bewilderment, and something of that same sense returns each time we re-hear these lines and re-focus their meaning. If our act of reading is an act of metamorphosing the fragments towards a whole, metamorphosis also belongs in the passage as a directly stated theme:

> *nel foco che gli affina*

– into the fire which refines them. This Dantescan fire changes and purifies – in a word, metamorphoses; and the sliver of Dante gives place immediately to another myth of metamorphosis, that of Philomela and Procne which we have already explored:

> *Quando fiam uti chelidon*

– when shall I become like the swallow? Eliot has already used Ovid's story in Part II, the 'Game of Chess' section; in these closing lines in Part V, it is the reference to the story in the anonymous, possibly second to fourth century B.C., *Pervigilium Veneris* that he fragments. Why he uses this half line, splicing it with a snatch of Tennyson, 'O swallow, swallow', I want to go on to consider. For the moment, I offer *The Waste Land*'s climax, as an illustration of my theme that by the twentieth century, metamorphosis has become a primary component of style itself. If this is evidence for the existence of that elusive 'spirit of the age' – in montage, collage, decalcomania, in Joycean word-play – the surprising thing is the variety of uses metamorphosis has been put to. My present and necessarily limited concern, however, is with Eliot and Pound, and at this point it must be with Eliot and principally some of the early poems and *The Waste Land*. I want to extend a line of thought first pursued in Sister Bernetta Quinn's pioneering study, *The Metamorphic Tradition in Modern Poetry* of 1955.[2]

2   Rutgers University Press, New Brunswick, New Jersey.

Eliot and Pound both respond to the idea of metamorphosis but in startlingly different ways. Pound still shares
Ovid's feeling that we belong to our world and of the essential
unity of men with animal creation. If, as Pound has it, the
poet's 'I' is to be confirmed and created by 'casting off [. . .]
complete masks of the self in each poem', for him there exists
an invitation to the dramatic and the creative in this process
to which he actively and willingly responds. For this process,
too, is grounded in a world of variety and fecundity. Ovid's
own ranging along the sound scale from bellowings, lowings,
sighings, hissings, croakings to speech and song bears witness
to this various world. The metamorphoses which accompany
these sounds may be attended by pain and distress, but they
are to be wondered at. Metamorphosis may demonstrate the
fragility of the self, but it also challenges the bullying
autonomy of that self and it relates all selves to a single and
miraculous universe.

For Eliot, on the other hand, a sense of metamorphosis
often means a sense of the provisional nature of personality.
If poems are 'masks of the self', Eliot's chosen masks are not
Pound's Bertrans de Born with his, 'Damn it all! all this our
South stinks peace' – or Sigismondo Malatesta or, as in the
Women of Trachis, Heracles. Prufrock has seen his head
'brought in upon a platter', but he's no prophet, no John the
Baptist; 'no Prince Hamlet, nor was meant to be'; he feels
more like Polonius, 'Almost, at times, the Fool'. Given the
imagination of metamorphosis, his thoughts would scarcely
run on tree or stone, bird or beast:

> I should have been a pair of ragged claws
> Scuttling across the floors of silent seas.

He'll neither bellow nor hiss: he chooses silence. The young
man in *Portrait of a Lady* feels driven to become a less
resourceful Proteus:

> And I must borrow every changing shape
> To find expression . . . dance, dance
> Like a dancing bear,
> Cry like a parrot, chatter like an ape.
> Let us take the air, in a tobacco trance –

And that passage, too, runs aground on silence in the form of a dash and a space of white paper, having traversed the subhuman possibilities of parrot and ape with cries that resemble language yet are only noise. Here, already in these early poems, Eliot's characteristic soundscape is taking form. It ranges from the silence that threatens to the silence that is fecund. It takes in subhuman noises and bird-sounds. It reminds us of the difficulty of saying just what we mean, and it holds out the promise of meaningful speech and perhaps song. The promise of song comes even in the legend of Philomela to which Eliot reverts – Philomela who has no tongue and yet can sing. Silence, speech, song, music. If this is an art that aspires to the condition of music – and *Love Song, Preludes, Rhapsody, Four Quartets* would lead one to suppose that it does – then it is a music listened for fearfully across chatter and troubled silences, a music mocked at by voices inside the poet's own head.

How differently Rilke's Orpheus in *Sonnets to Orpheus* proposes to translate the voices of the creatures of stillness – *Tiere aus Stille* – and also the bellowing, cry, roar – *Brüllen, Schrei, Geröhr* – until he has raised for this subworld temples in hearing – *Tempel im Gehör* and as he sings this world, it, too, will be forced to confess that *Gesang ist Dasein* – song is the there-being. Well it might be, one can imagine Prufrock glumly responding – he who never sings his love song; he who cannot say what he means but has heard the mermaids *sing* what they mean – for he has learned Donne's lesson, 'Teach me to hear mermaids singing', but realizes they only sing 'each to each': 'I do not think they will sing to me.' They sing with as little concern for him, as excludingly, as the voices of the Rhine-maidens with their 'Weialala leia / Wallala leialala' for the inhabitants of *The Waste Land*. In 'The Fire Sermon', Section III of *The Waste Land,* this chorus keeps returning in the wake of the words of the three Thames-daughters. On its third recurrence it has dwindled down to 'la la', as if it had faded out to another plane of being altogether, or as if the sordid happenings on Margate Sands had severed the Waste Land world from that mythic wave-length. Eliot's note points us to Wagner's *Götterdämmerung* Act III, Scene I, where the Rhine-maidens address Siegfried, speaking like the Thames-daughters 'in turn', as Eliot says. But what they in fact don't do in Act III of *Götterdämmerung* is to sing their 'Weialala leia / Wallala leialala'. They begin in Act III by lamenting that the Rhine is now dark because their gold has been stolen, just as the first Thames-daughter laments that 'The river sweats / Oil and tar'. 'Weialala' etc. is the joyful noise that *opens* the *Ring* cycle in *Das Rheingold*, before the theft of the gold – and before the pollution, that is, of the river. What is the meaning for those of us wandering in the Waste Land, of the joyful glossolalia of 'Weialala leia / Wallala leialala'? Apparently the meaning, spilling out from the Rhine-maidens' circle of exclusion, from the nursery noises of these eternal children at play is that for them, their gold safe, *Gesang ist Dasein* – song, in Rilkean parlance, is the there-being.

But the rest of us have our lives to live, such as they are, and such is Prufrock's that – is he speaking for his divided and thus plural self? – 'human voices wake us and we drown'. Silence, speech, song, music. What an ennobling hierarchy if only we could climb into it instead of always sliding back into the silence that threatens to rob speech of meaning. Prufrock drowns – 'we' drown – under a silence as deep as that in which he would choose to be a crab

> Scuttling across the floors of silent seas

– a phrase which itself draws on the dehumanizing threat of Tennyson's 'The stillness of the central sea'. We know what those 'human voices' already mean, or how little meaning they carry for Prufrock, in the much discussed couplet

> In the room the women come and go
> Talking of Michelangelo.

The women have been accused of having high-pitched voices (though Eliot does not say so) and of being culture snobs (though only literary critics could imagine the subject of Michelangelo as beyond the range of normal conversation).

Accurately, Christopher Ricks has indicated the words' 'tone-lessness' in this couplet.[3] And surely they are toneless because the ear receiving them – Prufrock's ear – is numbed beyond feeling; they brush against that ear as mere noise – not ape noise or parrot noise perhaps, but noise that excludes Prufrock as surely as the mermaids' song. In given situations, in the confusing soundscape of these poems, what is there to choose between noise and song? – in the situation, say, of the man in *The Waste Land* drafts like 'a deaf mute swimming deep below the surface' among 'concatenated words from which the sense seemed gone'. And appropriate to the desperation of this state of mind in *Prufrock* itself is that we get the foreign sound of *Michelangelo* – 'Talking of Michelangelo' – and not the more usual 'Michaelangelo'.[4] This, again appropriately, is a poem into which we have to battle our way through an epigraph in the same language as *Michelangelo* – an epigraph in which Guido da Montefeltro offers to reveal himself to Dante because he believes his words will never get back to the human world. Prufrock speaks on the identical supposition. That same passage of Dante is preceded in *Inferno* XXVII by stanzas which evoke Guido's difficulty in finding a voice to speak *with,* and at first he can only make crackling noises out of the flame in which he is imprisoned, which he has become.[5] It would take more than Rilke's Orpheus to transmute these noises into song. From silence to song. Perhaps we may gain a little coherent speech, these poems seem to say, but can we ever sing of summer 'in full-throated ease' like Keats' nightingale? Eliot insists he is no romantic poet, yet Philomela, the nightingale, sings for him the meaningful, wordless song that transfigures the Waste Land.

3   In a talk 'Tone in Eliot's Poetry' reported in 'Commentary', *Times Literary Supplement,* 2 Nov. 1973, p. 134.
4   In 'What Dante Means to Me' (1950) Eliot tells us that, as a young man, he read Dante via a prose crib and committed passages to memory. 'Heaven knows what it would have sounded like, had I recited it aloud', he comments. In his recorded recitation of *Prufrock,* he pronounces 'Michelangelo' 'Michaelangelo'.
5   See Michael Edwards' alert analysis in his *Eliot/Language* (Aquila, Isle of Skye, 1975), pp. 11–12.

However, it is all those noises that refuse to be transmuted into Rilke's Orphic song or Keats' 'full-throated ease' that make the soundscape of Eliot's poetry so distinct, when, time and again, as the changes are being rung on 'words', 'voice', 'silence', 'singing', our ear is brought up against the bird-noises of 'Twit twit twit / Jug jug jug jug jug jug', 'Tereu', 'Co co rico co co rico', 'Go go go go go', 'Quick quick quick', or foreign sounds that we have to scrutinize for meaning or the primitive radical DA, or the voice that says 'Ta ta', or the Rhine chorus snapped off to 'la la', or 'Drip drop drip drop drop drop drop', or 'Datta. Dayadhvam. Damyata.' which may mean 'Give, sympathize, control' but in the cataract of fragments at the close of *The Waste Land*, to a western ear sounds to be running back into gibberish; or

> Hoo ha ha
> Hoo ha ha
> Hoo
> Hoo
> Hoo

which – we are at the conclusion of *Sweeney Agonistes* – gets for follow-up not a stage-direction, 'A knock is heard at the door', or 'Nine distinct raps are heard at the door' but (in capital letters and measured out in verse lines):

> KNOCK KNOCK KNOCK
> KNOCK KNOCK KNOCK
> KNOCK
> KNOCK
> KNOCK

This recalls an identical device earlier on in the piece: the first time the word 'coffin' ushers in the nine KNOCKs, the second time the word 'dead'. So, confronting us with intimations of mortality, and repeating the same nine-syllable cadence as in

> Hoo ha ha
> Hoo ha ha
> Hoo
> Hoo
> Hoo

the nine repetitions of 'KNOCK', there on the page, recall to us the experience of gazing at one word, or of repeating it nine times over, and then realizing the peculiar way in which meaning comes close to noise when it is lodged in a single and isolated syllable like this.

With this metamorphosis of meaning into noise and the reverse process, amid bird-sounds – is there any single poem of the same length with as many bird calls as *The Waste Land*? – amid da's, hoo-ha's, glossolalia, snatches of foreign quotations, the ear encounters the soundscape of a world where metamorphosis invades and shapes the fabric of the poetry itself. This metamorphosis concerns not only the significance of sounds but the significance of things seen, thought about, remembered. They acquire dangerous powers within the mind. Landscape or cityscape is as full of admonition as soundscape. As early as Prufrock, streets became 'a tedious argument / Of insidious intent', the yellow fog becomes a big cat that falls asleep curled round the house; one wears a 'necktie rich and modest, but asserted by a simple pin' and the pin becomes part of the hell that is other people –

> And when I am formulated, sprawling on a pin,
> When I am pinned and wriggling on the wall,
> Then how should I begin [etc.].

'Regard that woman / Who hesitates toward you', says a street-lamp in *Rhapsody on a Windy Night*. You do as you are told,

> And you see the corner of her eye
> Twists like a crooked pin.

Eliot drops the uncomfortable association of pin and eye ('that ball / A prick would make no eye at all', as Hopkins put it), but he introduces on the rhyme word for eye – namely 'dry' – the contents of the memory:

> The memory throws up high and dry
> A crowd of twisted things;
> A twisted branch upon the beach [. . .]
> A broken spring in a factory yard.

They are twisted just as the eye twists. The eye is apparently forgotten; the twisting has taken over. 'Remark the cat', says the street-lamp just as it said, 'Regard that woman', and the repeated imperative to visualize leads back to the eye, to a series of eyes: a child slips out its hand to pocket a toy, just as the cat slips out its tongue 'And devours a morsel of rancid butter':

> I could see nothing behind that child's eye.
> I have seen eyes in the street
> Trying to peer through lighted shutters,
> And a crab one afternoon in a pool,
> An old crab with barnacles on his back,
> Gripped the end of a stick which I held him

The crab is groping blindly and the stress on anxious visualizing seems to be fading until we get a third imperative 'Regard the moon' and the moon 'winks a feeble eye' and we have come full circle from the prostitute at the beginning to the face of the moon. In the landscape of *Rhapsody on a Windy Night* everything turns into everything else.

If everything turns into everything else in an early poem like *Rhapsody,* what of *The Waste Land* over a decade later? Eliot, in the notes, introducing Ovid's account of Tiresias from *Metamorphoses,* Book III, says:

> Tiresias, although a mere spectator and not indeed a 'character', is yet the most important personage in the poem, uniting all the rest. Just as the one-eyed merchant, seller of currants, melts into the Phoenician Sailor, and the latter is not wholly distinct from Ferdinand Prince of Naples, so all the women are one woman, and the two sexes meet in Tiresias. What Tiresias *sees,* in fact, is the substance of the poem. The whole passage from Ovid is of great anthropological interest

and he goes on to quote it. It's a puzzle to know what Eliot means by that dead-pan remark about 'of great anthropological interest' as you embark on this urbanely told incident in Ovid. It begins with Jove's argument with Juno about who gets the bigger share of pleasure from sexual intercourse, man or woman. He says woman and she, the arch-puritan, denies it. So Tiresias is called in as arbiter. He has been both man and woman, though he has never been what Eliot makes of him, an old man 'with wrinkled dugs'. He has been man and he has been woman – on separate occasions. He turned into a woman when he parted two copulating snakes with his staff. Seven years later, he (or rather she) sees them engaged in the self-same activity, and has the sensible idea that if they are parted as before, manhood may return. And so it does. As arbiter, Tiresias declares for Jove's judgment, at which Juno strikes him blind. Jove recompenses him with the gift of prophetic vision. It is this gift of prophetic vision which qualifies him for his rôle in Eliot's poem – as it qualifies him in Pound's cantos, drawn there from his Homeric context. But very differently from Pound, the business of the double sex, lingering in those vestigial wrinkled breasts, fits Eliot's whole concern with the uncertain nature of identity where nothing connects with nothing. 'Of great anthropological interest', says Eliot the note writer, apparently secure on that far side of the divide from the man who suffers, yet concluding a passage – the largest note to *The Waste Land* – where he is urging us to feel that this shape- and sex-changer actually contains within his consciousness 'the substance of the poem', that this witness to metamorphosis, 'old man with wrinkled female breasts', 'although a mere spectator [. . . unites] all the rest'.

Whether one feels he does so at all points in one's reading of the poem is questionable, but one senses in the urging of the note the same cast of mind that can move in the *Rhapsody* from the image of rust clinging to a spring to that of a crab gripping a stick. For the terrible thing about metamorphosis in Eliot's earlier poetry is that, although nothing connects with nothing, everything seems to be changing into everything else, that all these things are identical, that metamorphosis is not variety and fecundity, but the phantasmagoria of a divided self, of a mind that contains and unifies and yet, in need of spiritual metamorphosis itself, depletes and dries up. The poetry seems bent on creating an appalling parody of Marvell's 'The mind, that ocean where each kind / Does straight its own resemblance find.' It is presumably Tiresias who says, in the first section of *The Waste Land*,

> Only
> There is shadow under this red rock,
> (Come in under the shadow of this red rock),
> And I will show you something different from either
> Your shadow at morning striding behind you
> Or your shadow at evening rising to meet you;
> I will show you fear in a handful of dust.

When one goes back to the drafts of the poem one realizes that this is the rewriting of words (another metamorphosis) which describe the end of one more Ovidian protagonist – Narcissus, or rather the invented Saint Narcissus in Eliot's own metamorphosis of him: 'Come in under the shadow of this grey rock / And I will show you' not 'fear in a handful of dust', but (the fragment runs) 'his bloody cloth and limbs / And the grey shadow on his lips'. Self-enclosed and self-loving, 'His eyes were aware of the pointed corners of his eyes' – strange the way this line swims within reach of the line about the prostitute's eyes in *Rhapsody on a Windy Night*. It is, one might say, the swimming within reach of other appearances, and becoming other appearances, that makes Saint Narcissus' fate more dire than that of Ovid's Narcissus. At worst, Ovid's figure simply loves his own reflection, whereas in one draft Eliot's martyred saint wishes

> that he had been a tree
> To push its branches among each other. [. . .]

> Then he wished that he had been a fish
> With slippery white belly held between his own fingers
> To have writhed in his own clutch, his beauty
> caught in his own beauty

> Then he wished he had been a young girl
> Caught in the woods by a drunken old man
> To have known at the last moment, the full
> taste of her own whiteness
> The horror of her own smoothness.

In a second draft, Narcissus is sure he has *been* a tree, a fish, a girl *and* a drunken old man:

So he became a dancer to God.
Because his flesh was in love with the burning arrows
He danced on the hot sand
Until the arrows came.
As he embraced them his white skin surrendered
                    itself to the redness of blood, and satisfied him.

So now we find him, martyred, 'under the shadow of this grey rock'. One takes the point in the lines about Narcissus as girl, culminating in 'The horror of her own smoothness', that self-love can also be a form of self-loathing, from which there is no escape amid the boundless lability of this protean world – a tree, a fish, a girl, but never a stable I.

Salvador Dalí, in a poem written during the thirties after the high Spanish fashion in a welter of images and entitled *The Metamorphoses of Narcissus,* also imagines his twentieth-century Narcissus as pursuing his reflections through a protean infinity. He, however, seems to find in this cultivation of delirium, this surrender to the vertigo of shapes becoming other shapes, an ideal of consciousness, over-populating the void of interior space until it begins to resemble a film projected at eye-daunting speed. Thus one becomes interesting to oneself at the expense of never in the Socratic sense knowing oneself or wanting to. Why not give up saying what one means since meanings are so betrayingly, temptingly full of plasticity? One has reached the *reductio ad absurdum* of Wagner's patron, poor mad King Ludwig, and his declaration, 'I wish to remain an enigma even to myself.' (*His* fate was the *Waste Land* fate of death by water.)

Narcissus proved a temptation to overwriting to Eliot as well as to Dalí. The blind Tiresias, however, was a good choice for the interior vision that was to *see* all this panorama of dread: he bears the physical evidence of his dual identity, but as a prophet he points outwards from his own psychic wounds towards human history and he can stand for something in the poet without the issueless 'dancing on the hot sand' that Narcissus seems to encourage. That 'something' has to be spoken, and the wonder is that Eliot ever managed to lift the morass of it into speech (let alone song), since the hell he must have inhabited for years seems literally unspeakable.

The pain which threatens human response in the poem forces on to the poet – and us – a sense of a possible range of response forbidden to the inhabitants of the Waste Land. Within the poem, and outreaching mere psychological compulsions, are images like that of the interior of the church of Saint Magnus Martyr, with its

> Inexplicable splendour of Ionian white and gold.

That that should be the interior of Saint Magnus Martyr, and not a flicker of the self-regard of Saint Narcissus Martyr, must have been meaningful to Eliot too. That inexplicable splendour resists self-absorption just as, on a different level, the variety of sounds resists the transmutation into Orphic song. It is this sense of resistances in the poem that, in the course of our reading, leaves us free from the idea in the notes that it is all going on in Tiresias' mind. The note may be partly compelled by vestiges of Eliot's 'proteanism', but it may also be the result of a nervousness that the daring fragmentation of this poem – a totally new artistic venture on Eliot's part, ratified and intensified by Pound's advice – might not reconstitute itself as an artistic whole in the mind of the reader. But the sound world of the poem resonates in all our minds, as it teaches us to hear according to an acoustic we did not know we possessed. Tiresias may (for Eliot) '[unite] all the rest', but his is not the only or the most important voice in the poem. That voice says DA – give – whereas he only says he has 'foresuffered all'.

I have alluded to the soundscape of *The Waste Land*. I want to look now at the elements of that soundscape, to see how the tale of the tongueless Philomela emerges out of its gamut of sounds and countersounds – of silence, speech, song, music. Speech and the failures of speech are associated with psychic pain in Eliot. 'It is impossible to say just what I mean!' Prufrock tells us. In *The Waste Land,* the theme of speech – the legend of Philomela embedded in it – reaches back to a number of anguished jottings in the drafts. We hear of people with 'dogs' eyes . . . heads of birds / Beaks and no words'. 'What words have we? / I should like to be in a crowd of beaks without words.' None of this gets through into the final poem, but its traces do, spaced, measured, heard against other possibilities along the route of this journey to an empty chapel where, after various kinds of silence, the grass is singing, to the shore where finally 'the arid plain' is 'behind me'. One is very conscious in following out the steps of this journey, of silence and of words in a number of languages, of bird-noises and song, and the way these create the structure and make it a structure of meanings once the reader's mind has collaborated in putting it all together, reconstituting even noise as meaning, metamorphosing fragments into a whole. Some of the words, like *'Frisch weht der Wind'* ('Fresh blows the wind'), belonged to song in their original context, as did 'O the moon shone bright on Mrs. Porter / And on her daughter / They wash their feet in soda water', though in that original context, the ballad 'reported to me', says Eliot, 'from Sydney, Australia', it is not their feet they wash.[6] Silence in *The Waste Land* is ambivalent, multiple in meaning. At the most basic level it is the typographical white spaces on which no words are written, and which are let into this poem at so many points. Thus in the first section one goes from the ecstatic moment in the Hyacinth garden

> Looking into the heart of light, the silence

on to the metamorphosis of 'Desolate and empty the sea' –

> *Oed' und leer das Meer*

then to the physical blank of white paper, before the poem cuts into the bitter comedy of Madame Sosostris, famous clairvoyante. And the physical blank of the paper images the desolation and emptiness of that sea over which Isolde's vessel fails to come into view. The German phrase, balanced on the edge of white silence, calls up those other German

---

6　Soda water was, of course, looked upon as a contraceptive device – at any rate in 'Sydney, Australia'.

words, previously quoted in the poem, the song of the young
sailor,

> *Frisch weht der Wind*
> *Der Heimat zu*

('Fresh blows the wind / Towards home') a phrase which,
cutting away from – it is a filmic 'cut' I mean – 'I will show
you fear in a handful of dust', has led us to the promise of the
meaningful silence, which is 'the heart of light', in the
Hyacinth garden episode.

Eliot's quotations are used with extraordinary accuracy. He
knows *Tristan and Isolde,* not as the man who can tell you
which is the best of fifteen recordings to buy, but as someone
for whom certain moments of the work say – and the same is
true of his Dante and Verlaine – 'Look, you are not alone in
your feeling. All this has happened before in other minds, in
other times.' The song of the young sailor is a case in point:
it is the one unaccompanied fragment in the opera; it occurs
in the silence that follows the prelude, 'heard from a height,
as if from the masthead' according to Wagner's stage-
directions; it has the impersonal freshness of a folksong, its
haunting, literally super-terrestrial[7] nostalgia is heard against
silence and involves 'memory and desire' (the sailor's longing
is for his girl). It is broken into by Isolde's 'Who dares to
mock me?' in the opera, and by the orchestra slicing off its
accompanying silence as this story of mortal sufferings begins
to move – at times seems to slide will-lessly – towards death
and transfiguration. In the poem, suspended in typographical
space, *'Frisch weht der Wind'* ushers in the fecund silence of
the Hyacinth garden, and its universalized longing isn't really
quenched until we reach *'Oed' und leer das Meer'* ('Desolate
and empty the sea'), from the opera's emotional low-point,
and the blank paper that follows the Hyacinth garden episode.
Eliot's sources are metamorphosed in their new setting, yet
metamorphosed within a continuity where longing reaches

---

7 Logically this should be 'super-marine', yet in the opera house, for all the
paraphernalia of a scene on board ship, the sound seems disembodied and to be
coming from beyond this world. One never sees the singer, but merely hears this
'Stimme eines jungen Seemans'.

towards a possible fullness, always threatened by feelings of desolation, as in *Tristan*. Both the threat and the fullness are measured by silence: on the one hand the nightingale 'Filled all the *desert* with inviolable voice'. Yet all that another voice can say is, 'Speak to me. Why do you never speak. Speak.' and demand, 'Do you remember / Nothing?' Out of the ensuing silence of white space, the manuscript had once read, 'I remember / The hyacinth garden.'

An episode which strangely variates upon that preluded by the sailor's song 'heard from a height' is Eliot's use in Part III of Verlaine's recreation of another auditory effect 'heard from a height' in Wagner's *Parsifal* – namely the boys' voices suddenly impinging from the dome of the Chapel of the Holy Grail, 'And O these childrens' voices singing in the dome!': *'Et O ces voix d'enfants, chantant dans la coupole!'* In the opera, these voices of boys impinge on the deep masculinity of the singing of the Knights of the Grail – and Verlaine's line beautifully recreates the surprise and purity of that Wagnerian moment in his own sonnet. In *The Waste Land 'ces voix d'enfants'* impinge on a very different song:

> O the moon shone bright on Mrs. Porter
> And on her daughter
> They wash their feet in soda water
> *Et O ces voix d'enfants, chantant dans la coupole!*

Then, after a blank space:

> Twit twit twit
> Jug jug jug jug jug jug
> So rudely forc'd.
> Tereu

Haven't we come down from the dome lower than from the masthead? *'Oed' und leer'* is desolate but noble. What of these bird-noises after the nightingale's voice that has been called 'inviolable' and after the equally inviolable song of praise of the children for the holy grail? Eliot suggests, perhaps, that the nightingale only says 'Tereu' because it cannot get out all of the word 'Tereus' and the Elizabethan imitation of its notes – 'Jug, Jug, Jug, tereu she cries', according to John Lyly – represents for Eliot a crude deformation of that inviolable voice which has notes in common with *'ces voix d'enfants'*:

> yet there the nightingale
> Filled all the desert with inviolable voice
> And still she cried and still the world pursues,
> 'Jug, jug' to dirty ears.

And the switch from 'cried' to 'still [. . .] pursues' in that, from past to present, turns the screw of continuing pain. Yet accompanying that pain is the memory of an inviolable voice and, within the drama of utterance which is the poem, and against that psychic wounding which brought forth the poem, presses the sense of a possible wholeness, a desire to rise into speech and song despite that wounding, that severed tongue, and, though 'rudely forced', to sing inviolable. After all, it is the 'dirty' ears – 'the dirty ears of death; lust' according to the passage in Eliot's draft – that can only hear the single note of the nightingale's jug and not the roulade of its inviolable voice. And so the sounds oscillate, in an uneasy state of metamorphosis, between roulade and twitter, between 'inviolable voice' and the deformations of 'dirty ears', between meaning and noise.

Still in the world of bird-sound – but moving now from noise back to meaning – it is the imitation of the hermit thrush with its 'Drip drop drip drop drop drop drop' which suggests the sound of water that could make bearable the rocky aridity. And it is the cock – Eliot's cock speaks French – that presages rain with its 'Co co rico co co rico',[8] primitive sounds that give place to that other sound and root word, DA.

In certain of Eliot's bird calls – and I am thinking also of a later poem like *Marina* with the woodthrush singing through

---

8 'Co co rico co co rico' sounds primitive and right, though, perhaps one should add, only to a non-French ear. The French poet Philippe Jaccottet tells me that there is more of 'Cockadoodledoo' – clearly Eliot couldn't use *that* sound – in 'Co co rico' than an English or American ear immediately perceives. The *coq gaulois* crows boastfully to the French ear in those sounds that for you and me and T. S. Eliot suggest in its *Waste Land* context a primal dawn cry bringing rain and a measure of release from and relationship beyond the tensions of the all-too-human.

fog – there is a hint of self-forgetfulness, a will-less surrend-
ering up of the merely human. One recalls the composer
Olivier Messiaen, to whom also *Tristan* spoke deeply, and *his*
desire to go beyond western chromaticism via the language of
birds, with his composition of an immense body of piano-
music based on an exhaustive cataloguing of bird calls. Yet
the will-lessness of *Tristan* and Messiaen's own dissolving of
will by discarding the tensions of sonata form and listening to
what the birds have to tell him are in many ways foreign to
Eliot's discriminative listening. It is perfectly possible to hear
in the song of a bird merely the song of one's own self-
conceit. If ultimately Eliot is to ask

> Teach us to care and not to care
> Teach us to sit still
> Even among these rocks

the will-lessness implied there is in search neither of the
ecstasy of *Tristan* nor Messiaen's subtle evasion of human
tension and pain.

I have spoken of the extraordinary accuracy of Eliot's use
of his sources, and nowhere is this more strikingly in
evidence than in the way he reverts at the close of *The Waste
Land* to the Philomela–Procne–Tereus legend in the passage
with which I began

> *Poi s'ascose nel foco che gli affina*
> *Quando fiam uti chelidon* – O swallow swallow
>
> [Then he dived into the fire which refines them
> When shall I become like the swallow – O swallow swallow].

Now *The Waste Land* does not need to be shored up ('These
fragments I have shored against my ruins') by a study of its
sources, and merely to demonstrate how Eliot has metamorphosed those sources could prove a mechanical way of
illustrating my theme. Yet in moving among his sources one
is moving among works of art that have made our civilization
what it is – *The Divine Comedy*, *The Metamorphoses*,
Pervigilium Veneris in its lesser way, Wagner's *The Ring*,
Tristan and *Parsifal*, *The Tempest* (a drama of metamor-

phosis itself), *Fleurs du Mal*. Sooner or later, if one hasn't already done so, one is going to encounter these works, and if one looks on Eliot as an exemplary creator, one is bound to notice what he did in re-activating passages from them. One might also even go so far as to say that you cannot hear the opening of *Tristan* any longer, or the boys' voices in *Parsifal*, without thinking of Eliot's now famous translation of those moments, even though the *Parsifal* moment is 'fore-grounded', as the linguists say, by isolating another man's words – Verlaine's – against the imitation bird-noise of 'Twit twit twit'. And that experience of thinking back to Eliot in the opera house pleasantly confirms his contention in 'Tradition and the Individual Talent', 'The existing monuments form an ideal order among themselves, which is modified by the introduction of the new (the really new) work of art among them . . . the *whole* existing order must be, if ever so slightly, altered' – a conception, one might add, of the entire history of art as one vast process of metamorphosis.

In realizing the accuracy of Eliot's use of his sources, one learns something of the continuity of men's attempt to know their situation, and one grasps anew the way 'the individual talent' comes into possession of an exact knowledge of its own situation – becomes capable of uttering it, stating it – by opening itself to the great past instances, losing and finding identity through the encounter in a metamorphosis of self. What the individual talent loses is the unnerving, unnerved sense of naked homelessness and lonely complaint. What is found is that human woes, though specific to oneself in the uniqueness of one's situation, are no longer homeless or condemned to formless outcry.

When shall I become like the swallow – '*Quando fiam uti chelidon*'? I don't know what sort of literary currency *The Vigil of Venus – Pervigilium Veneris* – enjoys at the moment, if any. Yet Eliot's fragment points us back to a rich poem and so aware has one become throughout *The Waste Land* of the implications of silence, speech, song, the source which also rings these changes, must be, if ever so slightly, altered, as in the more august cases of *Tristan* and *Parsifal*. It is in the final stanza of the *Pervigilium* that Eliot recognizes a forecast of his own state of mind. This stanza opens with 'illa cantat' ('she sings') – it is a bird that sings – proceeding with 'nos tacemus' ('we are silent') and weaving a way through 'tacere', 'tacendo', 'tacerent' and ending up on the word 'silentium'. This stanza, arising out of the legend of Procne, Philomela and Tereus in the poem's preceding stanza, comes, in its poised uncertainty, as an unexpected conclusion to this poem which welcomes Venus and the spring and is winningly humorous about Cupid and the virgins. Allen Tate, who translated the *Pervigilium*, says of it, 'Up to the last two stanzas the poem is moving, it has its peculiar subtleties; but it is not brilliant. In those two last stanzas something like a first-rate lyrical imagination appears.'

Tate's own version is a little stiff in the joints. I offer, in order to relate the poem to Eliot, Thomas Stanley's[9] sprightlier seventeenth-century translation of the apposite section.

> The warbling Birds on every tree,
> The Goddess wills not silent be.
> The vocal Swans on every lake
> With their hoarse voice a harsh sound make;
> And Tereus hapless Maid, beneath
> The Poplar shade her Song doth breath;
> Such as might well perswade thee, Love
> Doth in these trembling accents move;
> Not that the sister in those strains
> Of the inhumane spouse complains.

I must interrupt the flow of all this to comment that Stanley had got it wrong, or was following a corruption in the text here, for according to Mackail's text, the bird beneath the poplar shade *does* complain. Stanley, again, is hardly up to the true harshness of the swan noises among which the melli-fluousness of 'Tereus hapless maid' breaks forth, and which the original Latin stridently and forcefully mimics at this point:

---

9 See Thomas Stanley, *The Poems and Translations,* ed. G. M. Crump (Clarendon Press, Oxford, 1962), pp. 215ff.

iam loquaces ore rauce stagna cycni perstrepunt.

However, he improves as he goes on in these two final stanzas
– in his version, of course, they are parcelled out into octo-
syllabic couplets and thus unrecognizable as stanzas. But now
for the part which seized on Eliot's imagination:

> We silent are whilst she doth sing;
> How long in coming is my Spring?
> When will the time arrive, that I
> May Swallow-like my voice untie?
> [*Quando fiam uti chelidon*]
> My Muse for being silent flies me,
> And Phoebus will no longer prize me,
> So did Amiclae once, whilst all
> Silence observ'd, through silence fall.

If that strikes you as too briskly neat, this is what Allen Tate
makes of it:

> She sings, we are silent. When will my spring come?
> Shall I find my voice when I shall be as the swallow?
> Silence destroyed the Amyclae: they were dumb.
> Silent, I lost the muse. Return, Apollo!

But there, again, the hortatory imperative and the rather
jaunty double rhyme (swallow/Apollo) miss the tone of
fearful uncertainty in 'I lost the muse through being silent,
nor does Apollo consider me, look back at me':

> perdidi musam tacendo, nec me Apollo respicit

where one can see how the poet's fears for the loss of voice
must have spoken directly to Eliot with his own awareness of
the depletion of energies endlessly coming between him and
poetry, and also with that constant effect in his poems, right
from *Prufrock,* of the poem doubting its own capacity to
proceed, to spit out the butt-ends of its days and ways, to
unravel itself, to translate 'The word within a word, unable to
speak a word'.

> So did Amiclae once, whilst all
> Silence observ'd, through silence fall.

One needs a gloss on Amyclae. The phrase containing the
word reaches back to *Aeneid,* Book X, and Virgil's 'tacitae
Amyclae'. The inhabitants of Amyclae came, interestingly,

from Laconia. As to why they kept silent and how this brought about their fall, the three detailed explanations already current among commentators by the fifth century are of secondary importance here.[10] That the silence was ultimately self-destructive is what principally matters in our present exploration. A second gloss would also seem to be in order about a point that may already have troubled you: why does the poet in *Pervigilium Veneris* ask when he will be like the swallow and cease being silent, rather than when he will be like the nightingale? Perhaps urban and urbane Romans thought swallows sang like nightingales? At all events, Tate offers the plausible suggestion 'that the poet when he asks *Quando fiam uti chelidon ut tacere desinam?* is hoping that he may become, as the swallow, companion to the nightingale', Procne and Philomela being sisters (the *Pervigilium,* incidentally, appears to use the older legend whereby Procne is the nightingale). 'This interpretation', he adds, 'has, I think, little to recommend it; but the reader may take his choice.' So much for Allen Tate.

What T. S. Eliot supposed about all this – if anything – is an insoluble question, but what he got from this passage is clear. In splicing it together with 'swallow swallow' he links the Latin poet's gesture of longing for a significant music across the centuries with Tennyson's in 'O Swallow, swallow, if I could follow, and light / Upon her lattice I would pipe and trill.' He sends us back to the *Pervigilium Veneris,* not to worry about whether the swallow will sing as companion of the nightingale, but to experience the hesitation between silence and song, and the desire for song as against silence, overshadowed by the pain of the episode of Tereus' rape. We think back once again at *'Quando fiam uti chelidon'* to the moment in the 'Game of Chess' section and

10 These are: (1) They observed the Pythagorean custom of a quinquennial silence and an abstinence from slaughter of animals. Attacked by serpents, they were themselves killed since forbidden to kill. (2) They suffered the attacks of their neighbours in silence and perished because of their non-resistance. (3) They had, in the early days of the city, given frequent false alarms of its being attacked. The authorities forbade such alarms, so that when a real invader finally appeared, the inhabitants perished through their silence.

> The change of Philomel, by the barbarous king
> So rudely forced; yet there the nightingale
> Filled all the desert with inviolable voice.

Sir James Frazer, footnoting the Loeb Apollodorus, reflects: 'The later Roman mythographers somewhat absurdly inverted the transformation of the two sisters, making Procne the swallow and the tongueless Philomela the songstress nightingale.' Although Frazer gave poets much to think about with *The Golden Bough* – *The Waste Land* and *The Cantos* depend on it – and although he translated Ovid's *Fasti* (into prose), one sees from this remark why he never wrote poems himself. It is precisely the idea of the tongueless Philomela that speaks to – that sings for – the poet, once she has become the nightingale. For Eliot, inviolable song must somehow be possible despite violation, and despite the self-violation that preyed on him at the time of *The Waste Land*. Tongueless, or feeling incapable of words – 'What words have we? / I should like to be in a crowd of beaks without words' – he must persist through words to meanings and to silences that are meaningful and not merely the uneasy accompaniment of neurotic dread, as in

> Speak to me. Why do you never speak. Speak.

There is much ground to be covered after the final 'Shantih shantih shantih' of *The Waste Land* reaches out over the silence: the poem ends without punctuation and the white space now suggests, perhaps, the paradox of the emptiness that might become plenitude. But not yet. There is too much pain too close. Eliot will live for many years *'nel foco che gli affina'* before, in *Little Gidding,* Part I, he can say:

> And what the dead had no speech for, when living,
> They can tell you, being dead: the communication
> Of the dead is tongued with fire beyond the language of
>   the living.

'Tongued with fire'. The phrase, whatever it means now in Eliot's poetry – and it means Pentecost – seems like the metamorphosis of other meanings, meanings that have been lived through and beyond, and among which there hover the antitypes – the shadow of Philomela bereft of tongue, and the tortured 'Burning burning burning burning' of 'The Fire Sermon' in *The Waste Land*. But this is to overshoot my present concern and to anticipate my next, which is to place against Eliot Ezra Pound and, among other things, *his* use of the stories of Baucis and Philemon, of Tereus, Procne and Philomela.

3 Ezra Pound: Between Myth and Life

The poet, in the act of 'making it new' (Pound's phrase) is simultaneously re-living the past. He does so variously – through the language he inherits, through the masters he follows, through the myths which often anticipate his own themes and even his own life. The unity of European culture is such that there is an infinite number of literary situations that cause us to feel we have been here before. The originality of an author often comes to precisely this: his ability to make us experience on the pulses a multitude of meanings that time, bad translations and now the disappearance of the classical curriculum are distancing from us. He does so by imaginative effort – as Chapman (say) painfully struggled to rescue Homer from the allegorizing of previous commentators. Pound, in order to make it new, reached out towards the Greeks from the – on the face of it – questionable paganism of Swinburne, though Swinburne sometimes seems to have been of more use to Pound than the commentators were to Chapman. Pound, in a curious way, re-lived *The Odyssey* – indeed, from early on, he regarded authors, their characters and the figures of history as being possibilities for reincarnation in his own person. That is one of his favourite variations on the idea of metamorphosis.

I want to look at some of the details in Pound's re-living of the Odysseus story and to consider how his literary metempsychoses – for he re-lives many stories – ray outwards to touch on the legends of Baucis and Philemon, of Tereus and Philomela. But, first, by way of prelude, a couplet I have quoted before:

> Nor dies the Spirit, but new Life repeats
> In other Forms, and only changes Seats.

That quotation comes from *The Metamorphoses,* Book XV, in Dryden's supreme translation. The poem has there reached its philosophical climax with the entrance of Pythagoras, who adds to the theme of metamorphosis that of metempsychosis.

In a novel where a kidney is being metamorphosed into a breakfast and where, smelling it burning, Leopold Bloom goes 'stepping hastily down the stairs with a flurried stork's legs', his wife Molly exclaims, 'Oh, rocks!' when he informs her that the word 'metempsychosis' means 'the transmigration of souls'. 'Tell us in plain words', she asks and patiently he explains, 'Some say they remember their past lives' – though he seems not to understand that *he* is Ulysses redivivus. More lucid than Leopold Bloom, Pythagoras, on whose behalf Ovid speaks in Book XV, is said to have recognized on view in the temple of Hera the shield he himself once carried when he was Euphorbus at the siege of Troy. W. B. Yeats, in an early poem with the unwieldy title 'He thinks of his past greatness when a part of the constellations of heaven', appropriates the claim of the Celtic wizard Mongan about a previous existence:

> I have been a hazel-tree, and they hung
> The Pilot Star and the Crooked Plough
> Among my leaves.

The idea of metempsychosis was evidently in currency once more among poets and theosophists, employed with varying degrees of seriousness and wit, or merely as a handy metaphor. Even T. S. Eliot hints at it in dedicating *The Waste Land* to Ezra Pound, *'il miglior fabbro'*.

In calling him 'the better craftsman' in this dedication, Eliot, using Dante's words of acknowledgement to Arnaut Daniel, touches feelingly but lightly on a theme which can so readily transform itself into a leading motif of metempsychosis – Arnaut Daniel redivivus as Ezra Pound! Further-more, Dryden, Eliot and Pound stand together in so far as all of them (Dryden in his translation of the philosophic core of Ovid's fifteenth book, Eliot in *Little Gidding,* Part II, Pound in Canto LXXXI) achieve a peak in their careers by an act of literary metempsychosis, by allowing themselves, each in his different way, to be spoken through by the dead. The process is, of course, by no means a passive one: to adapt Sir John Denham's phrase on translation, 'a new spirit [is] added in the transfusion'. The passages from Eliot and Pound have received widespread attention and I shall comment on them only in passing. In the meeting with the 'familiar compound ghost / Both intimate and unidentifiable' in *Little Gidding,* Eliot begins by submitting himself to another man's metre – Dante's *terza rima* – and to the attempt to bring over an effect equivalent to that in English. His metrical concern is, you might say, almost a translator's concern, and into this translation which is also an original poem, through the metre and the phraseology, through the introduction of the familiar compound ghost, his identity wavering and changing, enter the voices of the dead – Dante, Baudelaire, Mallarmé, Yeats, Milton, Virgil. Few have written more penetratingly on this episode which so intricately combines metamorphosis and metempsychosis than Michael Edwards in his essay 'Renga, Translation, and Mr Eliot's Ghost',[1] where he asks, 'doesn't this section [. . .] enact the strange and partly shifting relationship of a poet to his masters in the creative moment itself – in the very act of making the verse in which those masters are met with anew?' A similar process is at work in Pound's Canto LXXXI from *The Pisan Cantos*, in an equally celebrated passage beginning 'Yet / Ere the season died a-cold' and modulating into 'Pull down thy vanity, it is not man / Made courage, or made order, or made grace'. As in the case of Eliot, the basis of the achievement is metrical, as Hugh Kenner has demonstrated in a subtle analysis of this canto, Pound running through a gamut of past metres

---

1 *Poetry Nation Review*, vol. 7, no. 2 (1980), p. 16.

including those of Chaucer and Dante, biblical parallelism, Cavalier song and Imagist free verse.[2] The famous 'Pull down thy vanity' passage is spoken, like the chastening words of the ghost in *Little Gidding,* by a mouth other than the poet's, though it is the poet who must give tongue to this voice. This time the voice emanates, not from a compound ghost but a compound deity – a strange mixture of Nature, Aphrodite and the Old Testament God. This last comes as an unexpected addition to the pantheon of Pound who had previously suggested that the Old Testament should be replaced by Ovid's *Metamorphoses* and told Harriet Monroe: 'Say that I consider the writings of Confucius, and Ovid's *Metamorphoses* the only safe guides in religion.'[3]

In *Little Gidding* Eliot writes (and with the appearance of the familiar compound ghost there the lines take on new meanings):

> And what the dead had no speech for, when living,
> They can tell you, being dead: the communication
> Of the dead is tongued with fire beyond the language
> of the living.

These lines might serve outside of *Little Gidding* as a commentary on the rôle of the dead and the rôle of quotation in Pound's own cantos. Of course, Pound over-reaches himself with this device of quotation, but the speech of the dead as embodied in their written (sometimes spoken) words can often with Pound, in the juxtaposition of even the most fragmentary quotations, achieve results of Webernesque compression and intensity. For example, in Canto XLIX, Pound at one of the still points of the work invents a poem in the impersonal mode of Chinese landscape poetry – 'by no man these verses', he insists:

> For the seven lakes, and by no man these verses:
> Rain: empty river: a voyage,
> Fire under frozen cloud, heavy rain in twilight.

2 See the analyses in Hugh Kenner's *The Pound Era* (University of California Press, Berkeley, 1971), pp. 489–92 and Donald Davie's *Pound* (Fontana/Collins, London 1975), pp. 92–5.
3 *The Letters of Ezra Pound,* ed. D. D. Page (Faber, London, 1951), p. 250.

> Under the cabin roof is one lantern.
> The reeds are heavy; bent;
> And the bamboos speak as if weeping.

And so it goes on for more than a page, the passage itself a kind of quotation from one of the great past modes where the deliberate expression of one's own personality was not the poet's concern. 'And by no man these verses'. When this motif recurs in the Pisan sequence (Canto LXXIV) Pound, the broadcaster from Radio Rome, is a prisoner of the American forces and identifying himself with Odysseus in distress. At the motif's first appearance, it is metamorphosed by the briefest of quotations from Homer: namely what the imprisoned Odysseus says to the Cyclops when the Cyclops asks him his name – Oûtis, Noman. The Pound runs

> ΟΫ ΤΙΣ, ΟΫ ΤΙΣ? Odysseus
> the name of my family.

I spoke of Webernesque compression and this is it. The snatch of Homer – Oûtis, Oûtis – Pound repeats with a question mark and then, in face of the question, re-asserts his own identity: 'Odysseus / the name of my family'. In this canto, where names are important, Pound – like Christopher Smart in the madhouse – tells over those of his fellow inmates with affection. At the next reprise, ΟΫ ΤΙΣ is preceded by the Chinese ideogram for 'there is not' and followed by the line 'a man on whom the sun has gone down'. That repeated snatch of Homer, that voice from the dead, is tongued with fire by its new context and by its reminding us of 'and by no man these verses' – no man, Odysseus–Pound is writing them now, as he re-lives the sufferings of Homer's hero.

This is Pound at sixty. But let us go back in time. The young Ezra Pound also felt that he was re-living, being taken over by literary characters or their authors. In an early poem, *Histrion,* with more than a touch of pre-Raphaelite uplift, the young poet declares:

> No man hath dared to write this thing as yet,
> And yet I know, how that the souls of all men great
> At times pass through us,

> And we are melted into them, and are not
> Save reflexions of their souls.
> Thus am I Dante for a space and am
> One François Villon.

Such metempsychoses are momentary, admits Pound –

> This for an instant and the flame is gone.

And then he proceeds, with a rather Rossettian glance at the philosophical tone of the *dolce stil novo,* to speculate about the rôle of the self, the 'I', in all this and the way the 'I' is lent to these 'Masters of the Soul' who 'live on' in it.

If Pound had not done better with the theme of the Masters of the Soul living on, the poem need not concern us. What's interesting is that *Histrion* – literally 'a stage-player' – with its stress on the way the soul of the player is taken over by his part – anticipates that other formulation of Pound's, the persona or player's mask, which governs his later methods and gives its title to the 1909 collection *Personae*. He speaks in his essay 'Vorticism' of 'casting off, as it were, complete masks of the self in each poem. I continued in a long series of translations, which were but more elaborate masks.' So Pound in his poems and translations wears the mask not only of dead authors, but of characters from their works and from history; and Browning, Odysseus, Sigismondo Malatesta, the anonymous author of *The Seafarer* and Li Po all live again. That translations – 'which were but more elaborate masks' – should have been a vital part of this process reminds one once more of Dryden, who also found his way to a fuller and truer self by speaking for the dead, for Lucretius and Ovid among others. Pound's first wholly mature book was *Cathay* – a book of translations from the Chinese, and the principal mask there for Pound is Li Po, the conscious outsider. Translation becomes now a means of extending, of consolidating one's sense of identity. It's not merely a question of the weakly expressed neo-platonism of *Histrion* where into the 'I' 'some form projects itself'. 'Casting off [. . .] complete masks of the self' implies an active rôle for the poet: what is projected into the self calls for an answering effort of the self to embody and utter its discovery. The dead must rise again in the poetry. Metempsychosis for Pound is a matter of co-operation.

So in the discarded first version of Canto I, which appeared in *Poetry* for June 1917, Pound enters into an energetic colloquy with Robert Browning and, in his search for the subject of his new and 'exceeding long' poem, he asks of Browning

> what were the use
> Of setting figures up and breathing life upon them
> Were't not *our* life, your life, my life extended?

That all this is supposed to be taking place in Sirmio on Lake Garda, once inhabited by Catullus – a dead poet whom Pound also engages in spirit colloquy – and that the day is Corpus Christi, are also important. Pound goes to some pains to create the processional ebullience of the religious festival in a bustling, rather over-eager Browningesque style. And, for all the immaturity of this first draft, how accurately his intuition circles round the central mystery of this day – Corpus Christi, the feast in honour of the consecrated host, a celebrating of transubstantiation, that Christian metamorphosis of the bread and wine into flesh and blood, that ultimate confirmation of the power of the risen dead. Yet for Pound, 'a pagan fundamentalist' as Robert Duncan calls him, it is precisely the pagan elements in this festival that attract him:

> Mid-June: some old god eats the smoke, 'tis not the saints;
> And up and out to the half-ruined chapel.

Eliot's vegetation gods in *The Waste Land* stir with intimations of a metamorphosis that is the Christian resurrection; the empty chapel there – he had already, incidentally, come upon his friend's 'half-ruined chapel' before writing his own poem – yearns to be filled with Christ. Pound, on the other hand, is travelling in the opposite direction: Corpus Christi stirs with intimations of the vegetation gods and the miracles of Ovid's *Metamorphoses*. As for the half-ruined chapel, it was Pound who said that if he had the money *he* would restore the temple to Aphrodite at Terracina and the

stone eyes would again look seaward. In the present poem, he
writes:

> Gods float in the azure air,
> Bright gods, and Tuscan, back before dew was shed,
> It is a world like Puvis?
> > Never so pale, my friend,
> 'Tis the first light – not half light – Panisks
> And oak-girls and the Maenads
> Have all the wood. Our olive Sirmio
> Lies in its burnished mirror, and the Mounts Balde and
> > > Riva
> Are alive with song, and all the leaves are full of voices.
> 'Non è fuggito'.
> > 'It is not gone.' Metastasio
> Is right – we have that world about us.

'All the leaves are full of voices' – 'for the leaves were full of
children': once again we track the Eliot of *Burnt Norton* in
Pound's snow.[4] For Pound 'all the leaves *are* full', not 'were
full'. We need not shore fragments of past myths against our
ruins, like Eliot at the conclusion of *The Waste Land*: 'we
have that world about us'. Pound is claiming that the gods
return as images of present experience. Eliot, so Pound might
have said, devitalizes the past with his 'These fragments I
have shored against my ruins', and Canto VIII accuses,
'these fragments you have shelved'. The gods need not be the
pale gods of Puvis de Chavannes' paintings, though, as
Pound wrote in a lovely early poem, *The Return,* that is the
bloodless condition the world of 1912 banished them to:

> See, they return; ah, see the tentative
> Movements, and the slow feet,
> The trouble in the pace and the uncertain
> Wavering!
>
> See, they return, one, and by one,
> With fear, as half-awakened;
> As if the snow should hesitate
> And murmur in the wind,
> > and half turn back;

4 Kipling's story, 'They', also seems to have contributed to Eliot's phrase (see
   Helen Gardner, *The Composition of 'Four Quartets'* (Faber, London, 1978),
   p. 39).

These were the 'Wing'd-with-Awe',
                    Inviolable.

Gods of the wingèd shoe!
With them the silver hounds,
                    sniffing the trace of air!

Haie! Haie!
          These were the swift to harry;
          These the keen-scented;
          These were the souls of blood.

Slow on the leash,
                    pallid the leash-men!

We must not let ourselves be diverted from the very real
subject of this poem by Pound's 'poetic' stance in 'See [. . .]
ah, see.' At one level, it is an attack on classical studies in so
far as they have failed to keep the gods alive, have failed to
re-incarnate them in our own culture. Lost traditions, lost
awarenesses, lost energies are what Pound – 'after strange
gods' in Eliot's mock – was in search of, for 'these were the
souls of blood', not for shoring or shelving.

When Pound came to revise his first version of Canto I, the
Corpus Christi celebrations were scrapped: the bright gods
and Tuscan were reserved till later on: what was retained was
the blood metaphor. The first canto was to consist almost
entirely of a translation – transfusion or verbal transubstantiation, as you will. In this translation by Pound of a
Renaissance-Latin translation of Homer, with Pound, as
usual, addressing its dead author ('Lie quiet Divus. I mean,
that is Andreas Divus'), the rite is a blood rite, to enable the
dead – but particularly the prophet Tiresias – to speak with
Odysseus in Hades of what is to come. Odysseus, one of
Pound's principal personae, stands now in the forefront of a
poem in which Pound is to go on re-living his story and
speaking on his behalf:

          Dark blood flowed in the fosse,
          Souls out of Erebus, cadaverous dead, of brides
          Of youths and of the old who had borne much.

Then we hear the voice of Tiresias:

'A second time? why? man of ill star,
'Facing the sunless dead and this joyless region?
'Stand from the fosse, leave me my bloody bever
'For soothsay.'
        And I stepped back,
And he strong with the blood, said then 'Odysseus
'Shalt return through spiteful Neptune over dark seas,
'Lose all companions.'

This prophecy was to fulfil itself in Pound's own case with a fair amount of accuracy, in his self-identification with Odysseus in the cantos of his Pisan confinement, and in the doubtful homecoming of the later and mostly inferior cantos, *Rock-Drill* and *Thrones*. Already in his *Hugh Selwyn Mauberley* the self-assured, insular and English voice that buries Pound at the opening sees him as an Odysseus whose literary voyagings are to be deprecated as the aberration of someone 'born / In a half-savage country, out of date'. In his prose, Pound calls Odysseus 'the live man among the duds', but he also states that after the unprovoked sacking of the Cicones in *The Odyssey*, 'Ulysses and Co. deserved all they got' ('Hell', *Literary Essays*). In *Guide to Kulchur* he reflects on Odysseus' 'maritime adventure morals' and tells us that 'Dante's Odysseus sailed after knowledge without putting his own will in order.' And this is an uncanny – albeit unconscious – diagnosis of his own deepest fault. The man who applauded Mussolini's 'maritime adventure morals' in the invasion of Ethiopia might have been thought to know with some part of his mind that 'Mussolini and Co. deserved all they got thereafter.'

Much in the early cantos is couched in the language of heroic myth and the autobiographical cantos sometimes use this language in relating the voyaging and sufferings of Pound to those of Odysseus. To begin with, Pound seems not to suffer at all. 'The live man among the duds', he puts the duds – profiteers, bankers, armament manufacturers – into a hell (as Eliot has it) 'for other people', a hell invoked in some of the crassest writing in this very uneven poem. The Pisan sequence changes all this. The re-living of heroic myth represents an idea that Pound, like Yeats, looked for in the modern world. That is one reason why the figure of metempsychosis appealed to both their imaginations. But for Pound, in the Pisans, a myth re-lived must accommodate itself to a range of diction that Homer himself might have hesitated to put into the mouths of Odysseus' men:

> Pisa, in the 23rd year of the effort in sight of the tower
> and Till was hung yesterday
> for murder and rape with trimmings plus Cholkis
>   plus mythology, thought he was Zeus ram or another one
>   Hey Snag wots in the bibl'?
>   wot are the books ov the bible?
>   Name 'em, don't bullshit ME.

Such are the voices of Odysseus–Pound's companions in adversity. And follows the Chinese character for 'there is not' and then: OÝ TIΣ / a man on whom the sun has gone down'. 'In the 23rd year of the effort' refers, of course, to the fascist calendar with which Pound eventually begins dating his letters. For Pound took calendars seriously – and this shows throughout the Chinese cantos – as a way of incorporating myth into time. The Italian critic Massimo Bacigalupo[5] has pointed to Pound's invention (half joke, half serious) of a new pagan calendar when he announced in the *Little Review*:

> The Christian era came definitely to an END at midnight of the 29–30 of October (1921) old style.
>   There followed the Feast of ZAGREUS [that is Bacchus–Dionysus], and a Feast of PAN counted as of no era; the new year thus beginning as on the 1st November (old style), now HEPHAISTOS.

And Pound goes on to detail the names of the new months and the new feasts. Interestingly enough, in the light of that discarded first canto, Epithalamium is the new name for 'ancient Corpus Domini, 15th June' and the feast is now under the auspices of Kupris – Aphrodite, that is.

Bacigalupo also reminds us that 30 October 1921, when the

5 See his *The Formèd Trace* (Columbia University Press, New York, 1980), pp. 33–4.

Christian era comes to an end, is Pound's birthday (he was thirty-six) and the day on which James Joyce's *Ulysses* was completed, a coincidence of some note for Pound. Like Eliot in *The Waste Land*, he was deeply in debt to the stylistic invention of Joyce's book, having read it chapter by chapter in Joyce's typescript. His own story of Ulysses–Pound was now decisively under way and into its splendid second canto. Here Zagreus (Bacchus–Dionysus) is introduced in a re-telling of Ovid. He is the god whose feast falls on Pound's birthday and whose energies are to second those of Odysseus in Canto I:

> 'From now [. . .] my altars,
> Fearing no bondage,
>   Fearing no cat of the wood,
> Safe with my lynxes,
>   feeding grapes to my leopards,
> Olibanum is my incense,
>   the vines grow in my homage.'

Canto II, of course, is an exemplary work of the utmost literary tact, but the programmatic Pound, Bacigalupo insists, 'believes himself a new re-incarnation of Dionysus'. And, one might add, with some justice.

For the energies of Dionysus, the hope of renewal seemed embodied already in Pound's discovery of the principal writers of a young century, in his completion of a handful of masterpieces – *Cathay, Homage to Sextus Propertius, Hugh Selwyn Mauberley* – and in that irreverent, intuitive exactness which was to prove capable of helping Eliot into the full possession of his powers through Pound's drastic re-shaping of the *Waste Land* manuscript.

I want to move now from that hard word which troubled Molly Bloom, back to metamorphosis pure and simple. I must necessarily be selective here. I cannot notice all the varieties of it in Pound that Sister Bernetta Quinn lists in *The Metamorphic Tradition in Modern Poetry*. My concern is chiefly with two of the myths we have encountered before – Baucis and Philemon, and finally Philomela and Tereus.

I begin with something Quinn glances at – Pound's *The*

Tree. With the publication in 1979 of H. D.'s memoir, *An End to Torment,* which re-prints *Hilda's Book,* the manuscript to which *The Tree* originally belonged, one sees how that youthful poem stands in relation to Pound's early biography and the biography in relation to much later work. *The Tree* was written for the poet and novelist H. D. – Hilda Doolittle – when Pound, a very young man, was engaged to her. It seizes on an intuition that is very precious to him, a quasi-mystical experience he seems to have undergone, and he embodies it in the Baucis and Philemon story. Despite a dash of Wardour Street in 'nathless', it is a far better poem than *Histrion*:

> I stood still and was a tree amid the wood,
> Knowing the truth of things unseen before;
> Of Daphne and the laurel bough
> And that god-feasting couple olde
> That grew elm-oak amid the wold.
> 'Twas not until the gods had been
> Kindly entreated, and been brought within
> Unto the hearth of their heart's home
> That they might do this wonder-thing;
> Nathless I have been a tree amid the wood
> And many a new thing understood
> That was rank folly to my head before.

You will have recognized the literary paternity of that poem – Yeats' 'I have been a hazel-tree' which I quoted earlier; though, unlike Yeats, Pound is concerned with metamorphosis and not metempsychosis in this piece. This particular kind of metamorphosis, celebrating an Ovidian sense of unity with things, is one to which he will return many times – most famously in the early poem *A Girl:* 'The tree has entered my hands, / The sap has ascended my arms.' *The Tree* was the only poem Pound ultimately retained from *Hilda's Book,* the typescript he bound for H. D. in vellum, and he placed this poem first in his selected poems. *Hilda's Book* is crammed with tree poems: Pound used to meet H. D. in the apple-orchard behind the Pounds' house at Wyncote, and they would also spend time together in the tree-house in a maple in the Doolittles' garden. She, even in old age, signed her letters to him 'Dryad', his youthful name for her.

To say Pound was a tree lover sounds insipid – aren't we all? – and to call him a dendrophil will hardly do either. But his re-living of the Baucis and Philemon myth, entwined with that of Daphne, resulted in a line of continuity within an increasingly fragmented *oeuvre*. Zagreus (Bacchus–Dionysus), the god with whom Pound identifies himself, similarly metamorphoses into tree form – into the stock that produces the vine. Thus the 'IO' of the cry 'IO ZAGREUS!' in Canto XVII is not only the cry that hails the god, but the Italian 'I' (io) that draws into a single unity the poet, the god and the experience that informs a poem like *The Tree*:

> So that the vines burst from my fingers
> And the bees weighted with pollen
> Move heavily in the vine-shoots:
> > chirr–chirr–chirr-rikk–a purring sound,
> And the birds sleepily in the branches.
> ZAGREUS! IO ZAGREUS!

Throughout the cantos – re-emerging after all the aridities and obsessions – there is an awareness of sacred places, specifically of sacred woods, reminiscent of the haunts of the gods in Ovid's *Metamorphoses*. They are visited by maelids – nymphs of the orchard – and dryads, and you will also find bassarids there – the maenads of Bacchus–Dionysus. These groves, as they impinge on the embattled world of the cantos, counter-stressing, however fragmentarily, Pound's tendency to a willed didacticism, seem images and intuitions of a possible wholeness, an attempt to keep that wholeness alive within a poem which increasingly refuses to cohere. Amid these groves water, light and air interact and the presence of such groves can be felt even in architecture: Venice, for Pound, in the splendid Canto XVII, is 'the pleached arbour of stone'. Early commentators took this to be a sign of distrust for Venice, a marmorealizing of the vital world. On the contrary, the vital, arboreal world lends a fluid life to stone.

To the question 'Tree or stone?' in my first lecture, Pound might well have said, 'Both.' In writing of our 'kinship to the

vital universe, to the tree and living rock' in the early
'Psychology and the Troubadours',[6] he seems to be thinking
forward to that marble relief in the building he so much
admired, the Tempio Malatestiano, where sea-swirls and
tree-swirls flow on the surface of the stone, compelled by a
common energy, the whole enclosed on either side by
pilasters whose stone trunks flow up into capitals that break
into acanthus and oak leaves.

The same intuition seems to prompt his poem *The Tree* as
that which begins the late *Rock-Drill* cantos: 'That you lean
'gainst the tree of heaven, / and know Ygdrasail', which in its
reprise becomes:

> 'From the colour the nature
>   & by the nature the sign!'
> Beatific spirits welding together
>   as in one ash-tree in Ygdrasail.
> Baucis, Philemon.

This is the beginning of Canto XC, the first of four remarkable cantos, that in a very mixed sequence, *Rock-Drill*, have
something of the coherence and power of the Pisans. It
continues the motif put into the mouth of a peasant in
LXXXVIII:

> Said Baccin: 'That tree, and that tree,
> 'Yes I planted that tree. . .'
>   Under the olives
> Some saecular, some half-saecular.

Pound's dendrophilia is hardly powerful enough to save the
cantos of *Thrones* which come four years later in 1959, but it
is still in evidence. His latest discovery there is the Na-khi
kingdom in South West China, and one of the things that
attracts him to the Na-khi is the vegetation and their respect
for it – willows, junipers, spruce and fir. Amid all this enters
briefly a new hero, Elzéard Bouffier, who set out to re-
afforest Provence with his bare hands, yet we hardly see
enough of him to give the sequence the kind of coherence the
mysterious groves give to some of the earlier cantos.

6   Ezra Pound, *The Spirit of Romance* (New Directions, New York, 1952).

Again one must go back to Pound's youthful days. The relationship with Hilda Doolittle had taken place in the outer suburbs of Philadelphia, Pennsylvania. The Sylvania part of it strikes one in her memoir and it strikes one in the Hilda poems.[7] It recurs in the descriptions of the Wyncote district in Noel Stock's *Ezra Pound's Pennsylvania*.[8] At the most basic level, and as in so many American urbs and suburbs, the streets of Pound's Wyncote were named after trees. Even the Philadelphia mint, where his father worked, stood on the corner of Juniper and Chestnut Streets in the city itself. Pound, recalling Wyncote in 1957, remembers his father planting pear, peach and cherry, and he asks his correspondent about the oak ('purty tall in 1900') and 'THE apple tree'. When late in life he is released from Saint Elizabeth's Hospital and returns to spend a couple of days in Wyncote, he goes out in the middle of the night in search of an evergreen which he and a friend had planted behind the church years before.

In her memoir *An End to Torment*,[9] H. D. speaks of 'the Dryad or Druid that Ezra had evoked so poignantly' in the Hilda poems; she writes about the tree-house in the maple where they embraced each other – 'no "act" afterwards though biologically fulfilled, had had the significance of the first *demivierge* embraces', she says – and in evoking the scene when her father, Professor Doolittle, showed Pound the door, she does so by recalling the motion of the tree-house from a few pages before ('We sway with the wind. There is no wind. We sway with the stars. They are not far.' One sees from this, perhaps, why in writing *The Tree* for her Pound should have taken off from Yeats' poem where the poet recalls being a tree with the pilot star and the plough among its leaves.) Here is H. D.'s evocation – what is

---

7 In H. D.'s autobiographical novel *HERmione* (New Directions, New York, 1981), p. 63, Hermione (H. D.) looks to George Lowndes (Ezra Pound) to define her as 'a reflection of some lost incarnation, a wood maniac, a tree demon, a neuropathic dendrophil'.

8 See Noel Stock, *Ezra Pound's Pennsylvania* (The Friends of the University of Toledo, 1976).

9 New Directions, New York, 1979.

remarkable about it is her sense of biographic and poetic continuity from the sylvan days in her father's garden, to one of Pound's most memorable sacred groves in *The Pisan Cantos,* Canto LXXIX:

> We were curled up together in an armchair when my father found us. I was 'gone'. I wasn't there. I disentangled myself. I stood up; Ezra stood beside me. It seems we must have swayed, trembling. But I don't think we did. 'Mr Pound, I don't say there was anything wrong. . .' Mr Pound it was all wrong. You turn into a Satyr, a Lynx, and the girl in your arms (Dryad, you called her), for all her fragile, not yet lost virginity, is *Maenad, bassarid.* God keep us from Canto 79, one of the *Pisan Cantos.*
>
> Mr Pound, with your magic, your 'strange spells of old deity', why didn't you complete the metamorphosis. Pad, pad, pad, . . . come along my Lynx.

H. D., like Pound, consciously re-lived myth. In her long poem, *Helen in Egypt* – 'my own cantos', as she says – she identifies herself with and defends Helen of Troy. In the memoir she tells us with naive intensity of Pound's Odysseus identification, 'His father's name was Homer.' In the extract I have just quoted she sees how the legends that sustained their youth in Pennsylvania are still those to which Pound returns in Canto LXXIX and in captivity. I have the impression that the lynx passage in LXXIX was more famous with English readers twenty years ago than it is today: George Dekker wrote briefly but subtly about it then in his excellent book *Sailing after Knowledge.*[10] As in so many of the sacred wood passages throughout the cantos, it begins at dawn with maelids – the fruit tree nymphs – consorting with Dionysus and the bassarids. But, now, the reverie opens out of a Christopher Smart-like naming over of myth figures and fellow captives:

> O Lynx, wake Silenus and Casey
> Shake the castagnettes of the bassarids.

Dekker writes of the lynx passage, with its references to Kore (Persephone) and her eating of the pomegranate, as contain-

---

10 Routledge and Kegan Paul, London, 1963.

ing an 'oblique and very beautiful treatment of a young girl's
fascination with sex'. If this is true, the lynx chorus bears out
convincingly H. D.'s sense of its association with those early
days in Pennsylvania, in its transformation of Swinburnian
paganism and the dated mode of the Hilda poems into something universal and durable. Here is an extract from this
extended section of the poem:

> 'Eat of it not in the under world'
> See that the sun or the moon bless thy eating
> Κόρη Κόρη for the six seeds of an error
> or that the stars bless thy eating
> > O Lynx, guard this orchard,
> > Keep from Demeter's furrow
> This fruit has a fire within it,
> > Pomona, Pomona
> No glass is clearer than are the globes of this flame
> what sea is clearer than the pomegranate body
> > holding the flame?
> > Pomona, Pomona,
> > Lynx, keep watch on this orchard
> > That is named Melagrana
> or the Pomegranate field
> > The sea is not clearer in azure
> > Nor the Heliads bringing light.

Here is Pound between myth and life, drawing together
the threads of a tragic existence; reaching back to the experience he had had in youth of metamorphosis, of a mystical
unity with the tree-world, the world of 'THE apple tree';
recreating the vulnerable sexuality of that time which must
have deepened the experience; and, before long, he is to
addresss directly the girl who shared the experience with him
in the words, 'Δρυάς [Dryad] your eyes are like the clouds
over Taishan / When some of the rain has fallen / and half
remains yet to fall.' Here is Pound, steadied against his own
wilfulness and rancour, by a vision in which youthful sex, the
tree-world, the lynxes of Bacchus–Dionysus bring quiet and
order to that endlessly exacerbated will of his.

It is the exacerbation of will and the will's attempts to do
the work of imagination that make large areas of the cantos

such tedious reading. Pound wants to solve the universe and then comes to confess in *Drafts and Fragments,* published in 1968, the last of the canto volumes,

> That I lost my center
> > fighting the world.
> The dreams clash
> > and are shattered –
> and that I tried to make a paradiso
> > > terrestre.

In this extraordinary volume of bits, Pound has abandoned both his willed didacticism and the pretence that the cantos could ever achieve an ultimate formal coherence. The poetry gains immensely: *Drafts and Fragments,* published after fifty years work on this 'exceeding long' poem, remains one of Pound's most beautiful books. Fifty years! Perhaps Pound's tedious stretches in this extended poem come to no more than the tedious stretches of any other poet who has laboured long but at *separate* poems – say Browning, Tennyson, Victor Hugo? I doubt that. The cantos fail – if that is the right word – for two overriding reasons: because (as Pound says of Dante's Ulysses) he has not '[put] his own will in order', and because he pursues to a quite unprecedented extreme the metamorphic style where the reader's mind is counted upon to re-shape the fragments into significance. The wonder is that the cantos succeed as often as they do and that, over decades, Pound can still convincingly link up his fragmented motifs, as my final example will try to show.

I conclude with Pound's transformation of the story of Procne, Philomela, Itys and Tereus. He first tackled this in Canto IV of 1919, a relatively early work. Like the Baucis and Philemon story, it reaches forward over the years: it becomes intimately entwined with the story of Odysseus' homecoming, and thus with Pound's own hoped for return from the prison camp at Pisa. Writing *The Pisan Cantos* there, the wreck of Mussolini's Italy all about him, the threat of trial or possible execution always imminent, it must have seemed at times that for Ezra Pound–Oûtis–Odysseus there would be no homecoming.

Let us go back to less desperate days, to that fourth canto of 1919 – a canto whose composition actually pre-dates Canto II where, as we saw, Pound could confidently identify himself with Dionysus. In his first handling of the Philomela/ Tereus story, Pound anticipates Eliot's use of it in *The Waste Land* and the contrast with Eliot could scarcely be greater. While Eliot is to seize on the myth to express hs own alienation, responding to the suggestion of the cut-out tongue and also to the promise of song filling 'the desert with inviolable voice', Pound places the story in a montage sequence with other myths, suggesting the metamorphosis of common themes by different cultures. The most relevant of these to the cannibalizing of Itys is the Provençal story of the serving to Lady Soremonda by her husband of the heart of her lover, Cabestan. Pound – once more he anticipates Eliot here – uses the device of a reiterated bird-call (Procne as swallow) to link the incidents, via name of child, cry of swallow and what the husband and wife say to each other. The Latin here is reworked from Horace's 'three times mournfully [she called] Itys':

> Ityn!
> Et ter flebiliter, Itys, Ityn!
> And she went towards the window and cast her down,
> All the while, the while, swallows crying:
> Ityn!

The poem cuts back to the moment before Soremonda casts herself from the window and her husband says:

> 'It is Cabestan's heart in the dish.'

And Soremonda replies:

> 'It is Cabestan's heart in the dish?
> 'No other taste shall change this.'
> And she went toward the window,
> the slim white stone bar
> Making a double arch;
> Firm even fingers held to the firm pale stone:
> Swung for a moment,
> and the wind out of Rhodez

Caught in the full of her sleeve.
       . . . the swallows crying:
'Tis. 'Tis. Ytis!

There is no reprise of Ovid's story until the Pisan sequence and this time we feel not only its metamorphosis across cultures, but within one man's mind, as it attracts to itself counterpointing themes that reiterate or ironize the distress of Pound–Odysseus. For Pound, now, there is no possibility of an equivalent to the grand operatic gesture of 'No other taste shall change this': often all he can do is listen to the meshing and clashing of the contents of his own mind.

In the Pisan sequence, Canto LXXIV, an attentive reader almost expects a re-play of the Itys motif via the sound of Odysseus' Oûtis, Oûtis: is this a prelude to some word-play on 'It is', 'Itys', 'Ityn'? Apparently not. Then when Pound goes on, within a matter of lines, to tell the story of the Aboriginal god, Wanjina, whose father removes his mouth for having named too many things, one similarly expects he will revert to the Tereus–Philomela story of the silenced tongue. He doesn't. At least, not yet. It is difficult, however, not to believe that all this was stirring somewhere at the bottom of his mind, for within three cantos it re-surfaces.

Now, in the early cantos, Pound has echoed and re-echoed a fragment of the chorus which immediately precedes the entry of Agamemnon in the first play of Aeschylus' *Oresteia*:

Helenaus, heleoptolis, helandros

Pound, in a context of destructive passions there, punningly refers this chorus to Helen of Troy and Eleanor of Aquitaine, both fatal women. Once again he is referring from one culture to another. The chorus itself means 'Destroyer of men, destroyer of cities, destroyer of ships'. Robert Fagles' Penguin version of *The Agamemnon* felicitously renders the puns into English as

Helen!
Hell at the prows, hell at the gates
hell on the men-of-war.

In Aeschylus this chorus is preparing us for Agamemnon's home-coming – he is outside with the unheeded prophetess, Cassandra, among his baggage. We know that his wife, Clytemnestra, is Helen's sister, so we must expect the worst of her, re-alerted by those puns. In the Pisan detention camp the chorus and its context take on a renewed life in Pound's mind. For one thing, he (Oûtis–Odysseus) thinks readily of that commonplace of classical studies – the contrasted home-comings of Agamemnon and Odysseus from the Trojan war. In this new context of the end of another war, Clytemnestra appears in the Pisan sequence as the destructive twin to Helen, boasting over her husband's corpse: 'like a dog . . . and a good job / [. . .] dead by this hand'.

In Canto LXXVII occurs a reprise of the theme of naming via one of the other prisoners and then the re-introduction of Wanjina, the mouthless god:

> and Tom wore a tin disc, a circular can-lid
> > with his name on it, solely:
> for Wanjina has lost his mouth.

There follows an Eliot-like stretch of blank paper and silence. Within a matter of lines Cassandra – she who has a mouth and a tongue and yet no one will listen to her prophecies – is on the scene:

> the wind mad as Cassandra
> > who was as sane as the lot of 'em.

A silent space and then:

> Sorella, mia sorella.

That Cassandra, silenced, unheeded in her prophecies, resembles Pound, is signalled both by the space and by 'Sorella, mia sorella', – 'Sister, my sister'. And once one has mentally translated the Italian one realizes that Pound's maddening habit of quite arbitrarily making the going difficult for his reader had hidden from one, within the Italian phrase, a fragment from Swinburne's poem, *Itylus*:

> Swallow, my sister, O sister swallow.

These are the words of the tongue-bereft Philomela to Procne, Pound travelling back to the poet who, as he said, kept alive a measure of paganism 'in a papier-mâché age', whereas Eliot with *his* 'O swallow swallow' in *The Waste Land* travels back to Tennyson, the poet of impaired Christian belief.

'Sorella, mia sorella' comes towards the end of Canto LXXVII. LXXVIII has a reprise of the Itys motif from Canto IV – 'ter flebiliter, Itys' ('three times mournfully [she called] Itys', as quoted previously) – coming almost immediately after the reappearance of Cassandra:

> Cassandra, your eyes are like tigers,
> with no word written in them
> You also have I carried to nowhere
> to an ill house and there is
> no end to the journey.

What is happening with moving implicitness in the Pisan sequence is that the theme of not having a tongue, the theme of Odysseus' sufferings and return, and the theme of Agamemnon's return (in Pound's case the question of any possible return is in some doubt) attract one another. In doing so, fragments of the themes are suddenly activated and, as in a work of music, come into unexpected prominence, grow out of and mirror one another. Thus there is probably another – if you like, musical – reason why Cassandra and the Tereus story confront each other in Pound's collage of motifs. For in Aeschylus' *Agamemnon,* when the captive Cassandra enters in the wake of Agamemnon, asking, 'Apollo [. . .] / where have you led me now, what house' (and Pound echoes that line), the chorus compares her to 'the nightingale that broods on sorrow, / mourns her son, her son'.[11] There is some justice in saying that Pound is being over-compressed, yet what is filling his mind and what brings silent eloquence to his allusion here was once, after all, the common property of all minds that had received even a modicum of classical education.

---

11 Aeschylus is using here the version of the tale in which Procne, mother of Itys, becomes the nightingale and her sister Philomela the swallow.

And the fragmented musical motifs continue to build up their significances as the sequence proceeds. The birds – presumably departing swallows near the camp – write out the notes of their treble scale on the telegraph wires in Canto LXXXII. This summons up the repeated cry, 'Terreus! Terreus!' Tereus, the violent man, leads now, by association, to the idea of war. War circles us back in this same canto to the beacons – 'a match on Cnidos, a glow worm on Mitylene' – that bring news of the fall of Troy at the start of *The Agamemnon*.

There is, of course, one disquieting thread that runs through Pound's remarkable recurrences to the House of the Atrides and the House of Tereus. He handles the resemblance between himself and Cassandra with some tact and with startling poetic energy. But the curious want of self-knowledge persists in this hell which is now no longer just 'for other people': the Troy that has fallen here is the Troy of the Axis powers, those prophecies of his that were ignored included the ranting broadcasts he made over Rome radio in time of war. Wanjina named too many things and had his mouth taken away. Pound, in his own life, was to suffer all the implications of the half-read wisdom of that image. His own loss of tongue, the aphasia – to some degree perhaps self-imposed – which overtook him in the finally acknowledged remorse of the 1960s, rhymes pathetically with the myths which had long moved through his mind and which, an Odysseus returned home at last to Italy, he must live out in chagrin and in silence.

4 Metamorphosis as Translation

I have touched already on the way metempsychosis – the word that puzzles Molly Bloom – comes, in Ovid's fifteenth book, as the crowning form of metamorphosis. The idea of reincarnation is one of the surmises, at least in the form of a metaphor for literary descent, that some of the most unlikely writers have shown themselves willing to dally with. Dryden, in his 'Discourse Concerning Satire',[1] delights in the fact that Ennius 'believ'd according to the Pithagorean Opinion that the Soul of Homer was transfus'd into him'; and – in the Preface to the *Fables* – that Spenser insinuates, 'that the Soul of Chaucer was transfus'd into his Body'; that he himself, John Dryden, has 'a Soul congenial to [Chaucer's]'.[2] And he lends his voice not only to Chaucer, in his translation of that poet, but also to Ovid, the celebrator of 'the Pithagorean Opinion' in Book XV:

> Those very Elements which we partake
> Alive, when dead some other Bodies make:
> Translated grow.

So the soul of Ovid is 'transfus'd' into the body of John Dryden. Dryden's pun on 'translated' comes as no accident in this context, where he is at work as translator and where – the

---

1 *Of Dramatic Poesy and Other Critical Essays,* ed. George Watson (Everyman, London, 1962), vol. II, p. 111.
2 *The Poems of John Dryden,* ed. James Kinsley (Oxford University Press, 1958), vol. IV, p. 1457.

implication would seem to run – a chief variety of metamorphosis embodies itself in precisely this art. So my final 'variety of metamorphosis' appears as that same act of literary metempsychosis, the translation of poetry.

In translating poetry you are either 'transfus'd' by the soul of your original or you are nowhere. In achieving this metamorphosis, our major translators recover, carry over and transform the energies of past civilization. By translating poetry I do not mean the merely journeyman efforts, such as what passes for Sophocles (say) in the oft-reprinted Penguin of *The Theban Plays*. I mean translation at the level of artefact. It will have differing degrees of fidelity to the original, but it must be achieved art. My own measure is not Watling's Sophocles, but (among others) Gavin Douglas, Chapman, Dryden, Pope, Pound, as I have tried to show elsewhere, in my *Oxford Book of Verse in English Translation*.[3]

For the great translation – and in what other form would one prefer to read a version of a major work? – is as rare and commanding as the great poem. To illustrate my measure one has only to place side by side, say, Dryden and Lattimore. Here is Dryden – from *Iliad*, Book I – Dryden, our greatest verse translator, as he describes the sacrifice to Apollo and the ensuing feast:

> Then turning back, the Sacrifice they sped:
> The fatted Oxen slew, and flea'd the Dead:
> Chop'd off their nervous Thighs, and next prepar'd
> T'involve the lean in Cauls, and mend with Lard.
> Sweat-bread and Collops were with Skewers prick'd
> About the Sides; imbibing what they deck'd [. . .]
> Now when the rage of Eating was repell'd,
> The boys with generous wine the Goblets fill'd.
> The first Libations to the Gods they pour:
> And then with Songs indulge the Genial Hour.
> Holy Debauch! Till Day to Night they bring,
> With Hymns and Paeans to the Bowyer King.
> At Sun-set to their Ship they make return,
> And snore secure on Decks, till rosy Morn.
> (I, lines 627–32, 643–50)

3 Oxford University Press, 1980.

Here is Lattimore in the climax of this same passage. He
certainly lays out for our inspection every word that is there
in the Greek, but does he achieve metempsychosis?

> Then after they had finished the work and got the feast
>   ready
> they feasted, nor was any man's hunger denied fair portion.
> But when they had put away their desire for eating and
>   drinking,
> the young men filled the mixing bowls with pure wine,
>   passing
> a portion to all, when they had offered drink in the goblets.
> All day long they propitiated the god with singing,
> chanting a splendid hymn [. . .]
> Afterwards when the sun went down and darkness came
>   onward
> they lay down and slept beside the ship's stern cables.

In exploring the theme of that dialogue with former ages a
poet is drawn into when he confronts a text from the past, I
also want to reflect on the relation between the man and the
moment and the way a translator's recovery of the past can
stand alongside the central artistic effort of his time, and thus
alongside his own best work. This theme will allow me to
consider briefly Pound's sequence *Cathay,* his free versions of
traditional Chinese poems, and its relation to Vorticism, a
movement mainly of the visual arts in London in the years
immediately preceding and during the First World War, with
its highpoints in the paintings of Wyndham Lewis, the
sculpture of Henri Gaudier Brzeska, and Pound's own
Cathay versions. The Pound we shall meet here is a different
Pound from the wrecked Odysseus of the later cantos, yet the
period – that of the First World War – is already creating the
disillusion whose consequence will inevitably entail that
wreckage. Why, at the moment of Vorticism, a work of translation should parallel the efforts of painting and sculpture is
something I shall also wish to consider. Furthermore, the
phase of Vorticism was a critical moment for London as a
cultural centre and there is a tragic postscript to any history
of that phase, a postscript which involves both the city and
the fate of Ezra Pound. So the direction of my argument will

be from a general consideration of the poet as translator to a particular consideration of Pound's metamorphosis and use of Chinese poetry in the London of 1913 to 1915.

I want, to begin with, to range over the subject of the translation of poetry and its link with the major work of certain authors. A first measure of this relation is the sheer degree of imaginative scope and effort it takes to recover a past work in another tongue – or, indeed, at the practical level, a past or *present* work in another tongue. For the practical level is where the translator must start and the first experience he undergoes here in confronting his text is that it immediately falls apart, Greek or Russian polysyllables becoming English monosyllables, rhymes losing their identities, phrases going halt that a moment since (as Collins says) 'in braided dance their numbers join'd'. The first experience on the practical level of the translator – whether of long past or of present texts – is not so much one of metamorphosis as of disintegration. He might, as he grapples with his chosen work, feel that Dante's voice were addressing precisely *him,* when in the *Convivio,* the poet announces that 'nothing which hath the harmony of musical connection can be transferred from its own tongue to another without shattering all its sweetness and harmony'.[4] However, in making that imaginative effort required if the translated poem is to find its true metamorphosis – 'transfus'd', that is, into the body of an *English* poem – the translator might gain courage from another voice, that of Sir John Denham in the Preface to his translation of Virgil, *The Destruction of Troy,* of 1656.[5] Denham long ago realized what scholarly opinion has been slow to grant, namely that it is not

> [the translator's] business alone to translate Language into Language, but Poesie into Poesie; and Poesie is of so subtile a spirit, that in pouring out of one Language into another, it will all evaporate; and if a new spirit be not added in the transfusion, there will remain nothing but a

4 *The Convivio* (Temple Classics, 1943), p. 34.
5 In T. R. Steiner, *English Translation Theory 1650–1800* (Van Gorcum, The Netherlands, 1975), pp. 64–5.

Caput mortuum, there being certain Graces and Happinesses peculiar to every Language, which gives life and energy to the words.

Denham knows that the imagination must find and use these 'certain Graces and Happinesses' in doing its work for the translator. In opposing the 'word for word' type of translation – what he calls Verbal Translation – he sees, with wit and clarity, what Verbal Translation must entail, whether you write as an 'expert in the field' or not: 'whosoever offers at Verbal Translation', he says, 'shall have the misfortune of that young Traveller, who lost his own language abroad, and brought home no other instead of it; for the grace of the Latine will be lost by being turned into English words; And the grace of the English by being turned into the Latine Phrase.' Our supposed translator – if he is any good – will find encouragement in Denham, because Denham grants the imagination its necessary dues when faced by that disintegrating foreign text. If he hasn't poetic imagination – if he knows in his heart that he cannot translate 'Poesie into Poesie', however deft he thought himself at translating 'Language into Language' – he may yet have the good sense to turn back before he ventures into this world of shifting shapes and changing identities. Because it will not be long before he realizes that it is *his* shape and *his* identity which are being called into question. The words of T. S. Eliot, speaking of Pound's translations, might give our translator a final directive nudge one way or the other: 'Good translation', says Eliot, 'is not merely translation, for the translator is giving the original through himself, and finding himself through the original.'[6]

'Poesie into Poesie'. Denham's words seem to be an echo of George Chapman defending his own translation of *The Iliad* earlier in the century: 'With Poesie to open Poesie'. Chapman brings me to my first example of the imaginative effort involved when a major talent undertakes to translate a major work from the past. What stood between Chapman and

6 'Introduction' to Ezra Pound, *Selected Poems* (Faber, London, 1948), p. 13.

Homer? The short answer is centuries. The rest of the answer is other men's efforts to understand *The Iliad*. For, as soon as commentaries came to be written on Homer, it seems as if the moralists had moved in – moralists Pope was still trying to see past in the eighteenth century. The legacy of the years and of Renaissance humanism was a poem where nobility was the keynote, where Achilles before all things was noble and not – as we should now admit – massively self-misguided, and where the diction of the poem must be adjusted to these preconceptions. Chapman's *Seven Books of the Iliades* of 1598 passively followed such requirements; then, as he tells us, 'the first free light of my Author entered and emboldened me' and we get ultimately the version of 1611, and for the first time we begin to distinguish the outlines of the Achilles we recognize today. To what degree Chapman, arrogant and wilful himself, achieved this feat through an act of self-discovery, perhaps not even a biographer could securely say. But it is difficult not to feel that Chapman's renewed assaults on the poem result in renewed inwardness, a sense of self that so totally transforms Achilles in the later version and takes him, for all time, out of the hands of Homer's moralizing commentators. The struggle with Achilles meant that once Chapman came to work on *The Odyssey* of 1614–15, he could much more readily rescue Odysseus from the moralizers and allegorizers, and dramatize through Odysseus' mistakes and final homecoming his own hard-won progress towards stoic virtue.

The imaginative effort shows at other levels in Chapman's *Iliad* than characterization and that this effort does not everywhere meet with success, that it sounds *merely* effortful, stays with one as a frustrating impression. What metre should one use in translating Homer? An English hexameter, insisted Matthew Arnold. A ballad metre, said Francis Newman. Alas, Chapman's fourteeners – presumably a desire to match Homer's hexameters with a longer line than in English blank verse – uncomfortably recall Newman's ballad metre and even Arnold's jest that it sounded like Yankee Doodle. One could hardly say that of the final version of 1611 which, together with *The Odyssey*, formed the climax of a truly immense labour. The fourteeners now read much more freely, though there still hovers about them the feeling that they are not the inevitable solution to the formal problem. Words must be found to block out those long lines and there are occasions when one senses a certain logophobia at work filling in the blanks. In the process of revision, Chapman will even extend 'Nine heralds' to 'Thrice-three vociferous heralds'. Yet, as Pope was to say, Chapman, despite 'fustian', must be granted that 'daring and fiery spirit that animates his Translation'. For at other times the diction, not wedded to a relentless ennobling, persuades one that an imaginative energy has passed into the metrical form and that Chapman's enjambements have become expressive – as when the old Trojan chiefs see Helen, and are forced to admire her beauty despite themselves:

> And as in well-growne woods, on trees, cold spinie
> 　　Grasshoppers
> Sit chirping and send voices out that scarce can pierce our
> 　　eares
> For softness and their weake faint sounds; so (talking on
> 　　the towre)
> Those Seniors of the people sate, who, when they saw the
> 　　powre
> Of beautie in the Queene ascend, even those cold-spirited
> 　　Peeres,
> Those wise and almost withered men, found this heate in
> 　　their yeares.
>
> 　　　　　　　　　　　　　　　　(III, lines 161–6)

Or again, when helmeted Hector is amused that 'the horse-haire plume' (as Chapman has it) frightens the child he is trying to pick up, he

> 　　　　　　　　　　　doft and laid aside
> His fearful Helme, that on the earth cast round about it
> 　　light.
> Then tooke and kist his loving sonne and (ballancing his
> 　　weight
> In dancing him) these loving vows to living Jove he usde
> And all the other bench of Gods.
>
> 　　　　　　　　　　　　　　　　(VI, lines 509–13)

And there follows his prayer that the child will be his equal as a warrior. 'All the other bench of Gods' is characteristic of Chapman's lively diction as are, elsewhere, 'belabouring / The loaded flowers' (which is what a numerous swarm of bees does); the sea 'spits everie way the fome'; and 'life puts out againe / Man's leavie issue.'

One sees why Dryden, exhausted by his Virgilian labours – his weariness shows time and again in his version of *The Aeneid* – should, in turning to Homer, have found new imaginative strength in Chapman's diction – for Chapman himself had shown a certain impatience with Virgil and declared of the latter's swarm of bees as against Homer's, on which it was modelled: 'Virgil hath nothing of his own, but only elocution; his invention, matter and form being all Homer's; which laid by a man, that which he addeth is only the work of a woman, to netify and polish.'

Chapman laboured to produce an *Iliad* and an Achilles he could believe in – his aim 'with Poesie to open Poesie'. Without that effort his *Odyssey* and his Odysseus would have been very different achievements. As it stands, it is one of the most remarkable long poems of the Renaissance, its readableness generated by Chapman's finding, at last, the right formal solution – decasyllabic couplets, where, when he feels called on to tuck in more piety than is to be actually found in Homer, he can at any rate do so at a convincing pace.

When Keats looked into Chapman's Homer what he looked at were parts of both poems. I do not need to dwell on their impact – the story is well known. What is less well known is that on *two* occasions – this and a later one – the fundamental impetus towards further creation came to Keats from reading translations. The second occasion involved Keats' reading of another Chapman enthusiast – namely Dryden and *his* translations from Chaucer and Ovid. The exuberant masculinity of these was one lesson he learned and – a simultaneous lesson – the use of a more firmly articulated couplet than he had been capable of in *Endymion*. Keats serves me merely to emphasize the salutary relationship between translation and original work. My immediate concern now is Dryden himself.

I have already given an example of his Homer. It coincides with that last phase of his poetic life – perhaps his greatest – the fruit of which was the many translations in his *Fables* of 1699. If one's experience of Chapman's imaginative struggle as translator is of a man 'coming through', seeing not only his subject but himself more clearly, the same is true with whatever differences of Dryden. His versions of Ovid, for example, show his release once and for all from tawdry Restoration ideas about women and he becomes, in *Baucis and Philemon,* in *Ceyx and Alcyone,* in the story of Deucalion and Pyrrha from Ovid's first book, a great poet of the tenderness of married love. There is a sense of renewed intimacy in some of these late translations which signals Dryden's thankful break from his former rôle as public poet and theatrical entertainer. Perhaps most tantalizing of all is his first book of the *Iliad,* written when he had turned aside from Virgil admitting 'the Grecian is more according to my genius than the Latin poet'. This first book promises our greatest Homer so far. Had he lived and gone on, as he intended, to complete the poem, presumably Pope's great but often Virgilian version would never have been written. The spirit of Chapman would have 'transfus'd' the body of a new Homer in the first book of which the formal rightness of the heroic couplet canalizes and refines that vigour Dryden admired in Chapman's own diction. Tennyson thought Dryden's first book greater than Pope's. The passage on which he takes his stand is the moment when Achilles is on the point of attacking his chief, Agamemnon, and Athena descends, seizes Achilles by the hair, and dissuades him. Tennyson instances Pope's couplet where Achilles has ceased his reply to her:

> He said, observant of the blue-eyed Maid;
> Then in the Sheath return'd the shining Blade.

'How much more real poetic force there is in Dryden', exclaims Tennyson, putting beside that this:

> He said, with surly Faith believ'd her Word
> And, in the Sheath, reluctant, plung'd the Sword.[7]

7   *Alfred Lord Tennyson: A Memoir By His Son* (1897), vol. II, p. 287.

The energy, which Tennyson admired, runs all through this first book of Dryden's *Iliad* and it goes together with an energy of mind which, as in his first book of Ovid's *Metamorphoses,* can view the actions of Jove for what they so deviously are, and yet balance against Jove's amoralism a sense of his awful majesty. Yet this majesty stays immitigably pagan. It refuses to take on that weight of Christianized nobility which baulked the Renaissance attempt to see Homer whole and which still hampered Pope. Dryden's first book of *The Iliad* remains one of the great might-have-beens of literature – for once, in dealings with Homer, the imagination has thrust Virgil from the forefront of things, and has not yet capitulated before Milton's coldly noble divinity. The quarrels in the poem, both human and divine, drew their energy from all Dryden had experienced of kings and politicians, and the unmoralizing drive carries with it the disabused clearness of mind that had seen through its own world without running aground on mere cynicism.

Another example of this same powerful trend – a disabusal with the public and a re-energizing of the personal world – had already revealed itself in *Sylvae* of 1685, and once more the new element showed in Dryden's dealings with past literature – with the renovation of Horace: particularly in his recreation of the personal, convivial and amicable Horace of the Second Epode and some of the Odes. This renovation of Horace was, of course, a trend of the age, and Dryden made of that trend – the thrust of a civil war and political disappointments behind it – a sharply defined means of self-expression. I cannot linger on this aspect of Dryden, because I want to place beside his break-through via translation to a new level of meaningful discourse that of another poet and near contemporary whose example was important for Dryden – Abraham Cowley.

In the far off days when I was at Cambridge, no one told us to read Cowley. We were put on to Dr Johnson's *Life* of him in order to study 'Johnson on metaphysical poetry', and one gathered that Cowley was a second-rate metaphysical who had failed at heroic poetry but had done rather better in his elegy *On the Death of Mr Hervey*. Some years later, I picked up a Victorian edition of his essays, and realized that, of the poems with which they were liberally sprinkled, all the best were translations – from Seneca, Martial, Virgil, Horace, Claudian. These centred on the private life and the withdrawal from the court-world. As in the later case of Dryden, Cowley's disillusionment permitted him to listen to himself and, once again, he did so not in self-absorbed lament, but by realizing that other men in other ages had experienced these feelings and that in making current their words he was finding his own. This wasn't the Cowley of *The Mistress* or of the *Davideis*. Looking around for more translations by Cowley, one saw why not only the convivial Horace should have appealed to him, but the Anacreontea, where we find the image of the poet as un-public figure, dancing or drinking with his friends, his mind on the present:

> Crown me with Roses whilest I Live,
> Now your Wines and Oyntments give.
> After Death I nothing crave,
> Let me Alive my pleasures have,
> All are Stoicks in the Grave.

One should, of course, have taken to heart what Dr Johnson said in that *Life*. He rates highly the Anacreon versions and says of Cowley: 'his power seems to have been greatest in the familiar and the festive' and: 'The Anacreontiques [. . .] of Cowley give now all the pleasure which they ever gave.' Clearly, Cowley was on the wrong track with poems like the unfinished and unfinishable *Davideis* and its epic pretensions: perhaps he is even guying himself when he says with Anacreon:

> I'll sing of Heroes, and of Kings;
> In mighty Numbers, mighty things,
> Begin, my Muse; but lo the strings
> To my great Song rebellious prove.

One of the songs that comes forth instead is the Anacreontic called *Drinking*. Cowley does not convert this charming poem into a Restoration toper's song, in the vein of Rochester. With something prophetic of Dryden's cosmic imagination

when the latter warms to Ovid's vision of a teeming and
miraculous universe in *Metamorphoses*, Book I, Cowley
brings to the familiar and the festive a brimming freshness,
an eager imaginative generosity. In the translation Cowley
attains a cosmic grandeur which eludes him in the theatrical
heavenly vistas of the *Davideis*:

> The thirsty Earth soaks up the Rain,
> And drinks, and gapes for drink again.
> The Plants suck in the Earth, and are
> With constant drinking fresh and fair,
> The Sea it self, which one would think
> Should have but little need of Drink,
> Drinks ten thousand Rivers up,
> So fill'd that they o'erflow the Cup.
> The busie Sun (and one would guess
> By's drunken fiery face no less)
> Drinks up the Sea, and when h'as done,
> The Moon and Stars drink up the Sun.
> They drink and dance by their own light,
> They drink and revel all the night.
> Nothing in Nature's Sober found,
> But an Eternal Health goes round.
> Fill up the Bowl then, fill it high,
> Fill all the Glasses there, for why
> Should every Creature drink but I,
> Why, Man of Morals, tell me why?

It's surely right that the translator of these lines should have
produced as his masterstroke an imitation of Horace's tale of
the town and country mouse – a poem, that is to say, which is
light in tone and yet whose lightness does not obscure the
theme of being true to oneself in accepting the common
luxuries of life:

> Fitches and Beans, Peason, and Oats, and Wheat,
> And a large Chestnut, the delicious Meat
> Which Jove himself, were he a Mouse, would eat

– this being set against the restless urging of the town mouse:

> Let savage Beasts lodge in a Country Den,
> You should see Towns, and Manners know, and Men;
> And taste the gen'rous Luxury of the Court,
> Where all the Mice of Quality resort.

The Country Mouse seems to me Cowley's finest single poem. It is translation but with a good deal of latitude. The tale is told at far greater length than Horace's tale, yet it is the perfect example of the translation of Horace's manner into English. One might almost say this is a Horatian poem that Horace never wrote, yet one in which his spirit transfused that of an English poet and saved him from pretension and from the dispersal of his genuine self and energies. This is a major example of (in Eliot's words) 'the translator [. . .] giving the original through himself, and finding himself through the original'.

Civilizations tend to become ingrown and cease to hear the voices of previous eras except in their own reduced vocal range. This has been – often unjustly, I think – one of the complaints against Pope's Homer. The *Times Literary Supplement* reviewer in welcoming Lattimore's Homer – 'as crystal clear', he writes 'as a mountain stream; yet [. . . with] its sources in no English hills' – pauses to say of Pope's Homer that it 'was produced for educated *cognoscenti,* and merely reflected the poetic fashions of the day'. One can challenge this inane demotion of Pope by turning to a characteristic passage – say the attack on Achilles by the River Scamander, with all those kinetic verbs, all those hurryings forward across the couplets that so energetically fulfil Pope's stated aim: 'to keep alive that spirit and fire which makes [Homer's] chief character':

> Now bursting on his Head with thund'ring Sound,
> The falling Deluge whelms the Hero round:
> His loaded Shield bends to the rushing Tide;
> His Feet, upborn, scarce the strong Flood divide,
> Slidd'ring, and stagg'ring. On the Border stood
> A spreading Elm, that overhung the Flood;
> He seiz'd a bending Bough, his Steps to stay;
> The Plant uprooted to his Weight gave way,
> Heaving the Bank, and undermining all;
> Loud flash the Waters to the rushing Fall
> Of the thick Foliage. The large Trunk display'd
> Bridg'd the rough Flood across: The Hero stay'd
> On this his Weight, and rais'd upon his Hand,

Leap'd from the Chanel, and regain'd the Land.
Then blacken'd the wild Waves; the Murmur rose,
The God pursues, a huger Billow throws,
And bursts the Bank, ambitious to destroy
The Man whose Fury is the Fate of Troy.
He, like the warlike Eagle speeds his Pace,
(Swiftest and strongest of th' aerial Race)
Far as a Spear can fly, Achilles springs
At every Bound; His clanging Armour rings:
Now here, now there, he turns on ev'ry side,
And winds his Course before the following Tide.

(XXI, lines 263–86)

When a recent theorist of translation, L. G. Kelly in his book *The True Interpreter*,[8] turns for once to look at a major example of the art, all he can summon up faced with Pope's *Iliad* is: 'This is Homer in a powdered wig declaiming in a baroque theatre.' Pope, one must begin by admitting, had trouble with the simplicities of Homer and some of the 'lower' vocabulary, since his own diction is often extremely elevated and not easy to descend from. The kind of difficulty shows in a letter from one of his collaborators, Fenton, to his other collaborator, Broome – the *Odyssey*, unlike the *Iliad* which was all Pope's work, being shared out among the three of them. Fenton is worried at the prospect of Book XX of the *Odyssey*, where all sorts of low words occur. He writes despondently: 'How shall I get over the bitch and her puppies, the roasting of the black puddings [. . .] and the cowheel that was thrown at Ulysses' head, I know not.' In the event, Fenton made the bitch into a 'mother-mastiff', the black puddings into 'sav'ry cates' and the cow-heel became 'That sinewy fragment [. . .] / Where to the pastern-bone by nerves combin'd / The well-horn'd foot indissolubly join'd.' But Fenton was not the happiest of Pope's collaborators, being capable of couplets like:

Rolling convulsive on the floor is seen
The piteous object of a prostrate Queen.

8 Basil Blackwell, Oxford, 1979.

Pope works at a different level from that. His *Iliad* is one of the great translations and so, more fragmentarily, is the *Odyssey*. We are still being told, this time by a contemporary English poet, Norman Nicholson, in his selection of Cowper's poems, that Pope reduces Homer to porcelain and cameos.[9] When Pope in part fails, as in a sometimes unwieldy diction or his creation of a Jupiter who stands too close to Milton's God in *Paradise Lost* for comfort, his failure is on a more august level than that of producing cameos. His successes are magnificent and unparalleled – among them at times (and this surprisingly) an unexpected fidelity, which resembles Pound's, to the irreducibly foreign and distant. Unlike Pound, Pope did not always find it easy to allow this to show through, and one of the incidental dramas of his Homer occurs in the way his notes are often at variance with his text. Frequently the notes register something which is palpably there in Homer, yet has to be smoothed over, made a little more abstract in Pope's poem in order to satisfy Augustan and Virgilian notions of high seriousness. Yet this is not always so. And sometimes Pope succeeds where you might least expect it – in his awareness of Greek barbarity, an awareness that over a century later seems to have eluded Matthew Arnold in his *On Translating Homer*. What eluded Arnold and what Pope could see had to be recovered; and it was recovered, not by nineteenth-century British Hellenism, but in Germany and by Nietzsche. Pope perhaps would have recognized what Nietzsche meant when he spoke of 'the contradictions inherent in the Homeric world, so marvellous on the one hand, so ghastly and brutal on the other'. For Pope has a footnote of his own – these notes are another brilliant aspect of his translation – in which he mocks the idealizing of the Greeks by Madame D'Acier, an earlier French translator and commentator. The Greeks, Pope points out, were in the habit of slaughtering all enemy males and transporting their females into slavery. An example I want to quote from Pope comes not in the *Iliad* but from

9 *A Choice of William Cowper's Verse* (Faber, London, 1975).

Book XXII of the *Odyssey,* one of the books where Pope himself was in sole charge. This passage describes the punishment of Penelope's faithless women-servants and of Melanthius, who had previously insulted the disguised Ulysses. The relentless march of the couplets here – and on other occasions Pope can attune his couplets to tenderness or to a biblical nobility of phrase – the snap of the rhymes, the refusal to be diverted into moralizing comment, that favourite device of the Renaissance and Augustan translator, all these result in a verse that catches the unfeeling barbarity of the episode, verse at a far remove from those Ovidian graces with which Pope sometimes softens Homer's style. The speaker in this passage is Ulysses' son, Telemachus. He reflects on how the women-servants, who have lain with Penelope's suitors, should be executed:

> Then thus the Prince. To these shall we afford
> A fate so pure, as by the martial sword?
> To these, the nightly prostitutes to shame,
> And base revilers of our house and name?
>   Thus speaking, on the circling wall he strung
> A ship's tough cable, from a column hung;
> Near the high top he strain'd it strongly round,
> Whence no contending foot could reach the ground.
> Their heads above, connected in a row,
> They beat the air with quiv'ring feet below;
> Thus on some tree hung struggling in the snare,
> The doves or thrushes flap their wings in air.
> Soon fled the soul impure, and left behind
> The empty corse to waver with the wind.
>   Then forth they led Melanthius, and began
> Their bloody work: They lopp'd away the man,
> Morsel for dogs! then trimm'd with brazen shears
> The wretch, and shorten'd of his nose and ears;
> His hands and feet last felt the cruel steel:
> He roar'd, and torments gave his soul to hell –
>   They wash, and to Ulysses take their way;
> So ends the bloody business of the day
>   (XXII, lines 495–516)

William Cowper, tackling that same passage some sixty years later, in a version of the *Odyssey* which is often powerfully translated, allows the edge to be taken off the blatant barbarity there by giving the episode a kind of Miltonic lift, the gust of his cadence carrying with it a movement that is half righteous indignation, half shocked sensibility, quite foreign to Homer and to Pope's hold there on the ghastly and the brutal.

One does not, of course, undertake translation merely to show how different other cultures are, or to give barbarism an airing. The eighteenth century found Horace so appealing because of the degree of poetic civilization he represented – a fineness of balance, insight and wit that they felt to be recoverable and necessary in a civilization like that of eighteenth-century England with its own daily barbarities which needed tempering. This desire to transmit the strengths of another literary civilization is something one experiences right through the history of translation. It shows the historic instinct of translators as they operate in a given civilization and at a given time.

Translation requires, then, basically two things – the man and the moment: a man like Ezra Pound, for example, and a moment like the year 1913 when the widow of Ernest Fenollosa sent Pound her deceased husband's notebooks, containing very literal translations from Chinese and Japanese. What translation has too often implied, instead of the marvellously right choice of the intelligent Mary Fenollosa, who herself spotted Pound because of a group of his poems in *Poetry* magazine, is that someone is commissioned by Penguin Books to translate (say) Sophocles, someone who has never written a line of verse in his life. The verse of Pound's *Cathay,* published in 1915,[10] translates 'Poesie into Poesie' and in a way in which Chinese poetry had never before been rendered into English. As in Pound's *Lament of the Frontier Guard*:

> By the North Gate, the wind blows full of sand,
> Lonely from the beginning of time until now!
> Trees fall, the grass goes yellow with autumn.

10   *Selected Poems*, p. 132.

I climb the towers and towers
  to watch out the barbarous land:
Desolate castle, the sky, the wide desert.
There is no wall left to this village.
Bones white with a thousand frosts,
High heaps, covered with trees and grass;
Who brought this to pass?
Who has brought the flaming imperial anger?
Who has brought the army with drums and kettle-drums?
Barbarous kings.
A gracious spring, turned to blood-ravenous autumn,
A turmoil of wars-men, spread over the middle kingdom,
Three hundred and sixty thousand,
And sorrow, sorrow like rain.
Sorrow to go, and sorrow, sorrow returning.
Desolate, desolate fields,
And no children of warfare upon them,
  No longer the men of offence and defence.
Ah, how shall you know the dreary sorrow at the North
                                 Gate,
With Rihaku's name forgotten,
And we guardsmen fed to the tigers.

One measures that as poetry and not for its suitability as a
crib to the works of Li Po. For that purpose it is hardly
usable, though Arthur Waley, who also translated Li Po and
rather disapproved of Pound's attempt, was not above
stealing a line here and there to grace his supposedly more
literal rendering. What Waley, with unfailing instinct, does is
to sacrifice the finesse of that ear which, with Pound, was 'so
close to the mind it [*was*] the mind's, that it [had] the mind's
speed', in Charles Olson's phrase.[11]

In his study *Ezra Pound's Cathay*,[12] Wai-lim Yip tellingly
places side by side with Waley the poignant line from Pound's
version of Li Po's *The River Merchant's Wife:* 'Called to a
thousand times, I never looked back'. Waley dents that, so to
speak, to make it look like all his own work; he writes:

    Called to, a thousand times, I did not turn.

11 Charles Olson, *Projective Verse* (Totem Press, 1959), p. 5.
12 Wai-lim Yip, *Ezra Pound's Cathay* (Princeton University Press, New
    Jersey, 1969), p. 89.

The same poem, in Pound, opens with the woman saying: 'While my hair was still cut straight across my forehead'. Wai-lim Yip shows us Waley muffing this clear line about the girl's fringe with: 'Soon after I wore my hair covering my forehead.'

The surprising thing about Pound is that, at the stage of *Cathay,* knowing no Chinese, prompted only by the notes of Ernest Fenollosa, faced by a poetry without articles before its nouns, without cases, genders, tenses, he should have intuited so much about the nature of Chinese and primarily its use of the single line placed dramatically against the next single line, an effect that Waley's translations with their busy syntax sometimes tend to cancel out. It is Pound's sense of the effect of the line unit that puts him, with *Cathay,* into that select band of translator-poets whose work – and here I revert to a theme I have already glanced at – re-incorporates a past civilization into the central artistic effort of their time. Let me illustrate, with one of the briefer *Cathay* poems, this *paratactic* – one thing placed *beside* another – as distinct from *syntactic* drama – one thing fluently *linked* to another. There is the tiny poem, Li Po's *The Jewel Stair's Grievance,* one of those many traditional poems of disappointed love:

> The jewelled steps are already wet with dew,
> It is so late that the dew soaks my gauze stockings,
> And I let down the crystal curtain
> And I watch the moon through the clear autumn.

How often, in *Cathay,* as in poems like this, one feels that Pound's mastery comes from the way he handles the single line unit (as Waley rarely could) and the inevitability of cadence he can bring to it: there is *Lament of the Frontier Guard* with its:

> A gracious spring, turned to blood-ravenous autumn

or (in the same poem):

> I climb the towers and towers
>   to watch out the barbarous land

or in *South-Folk in Cold Country,* where the single line is broken down into montage:

Surprised. Desert turmoil. Sea sun.

Or again in the same poem, the montage of the two neigh-
bouring lines:

Flying snow bewilders the barbarian heaven.
Lice swarm like ants over our accoutrements.

Donald Davie, in *Ezra Pound, Poet as Sculptor,*[13] was surely
the first critic to see what was at work in instances like these
when he writes:

The poem establishes a convention by which the gauge of a
poetic line is not the number of syllables or of stressed
syllables or of metrical feet, but the fulfilment of the
simple grammatical unit, the sentence.

I began by referring to the man and the moment. Here we
have the man *making* the moment, the moment and also the
future. For, from Pound's moment of discovery, the writer's
attention is to continue to rest on the line as poetic unit – as
in William Carlos Williams, in George Oppen and in the
Black Mountain poets. As Davie proceeds to say: 'It was only
when the line was considered as the unit of composition, as it
was by Pound in *Cathay,* that there emerged the possibility
of "breaking" the line, of disrupting it from within, by
throwing weight upon the smaller units within the line'. One
of the examples he gives is from the poem *The Bowmen of
Shu* – that superbly fractured line:

Horses, his horses even, are tired. They were strong.

In the rhythmical pauses of that line, any mere purposes of
translation as crib have been surpassed: that line contains the
rhythmic direction of much later poetry – by Pound and by
others. Davie points us back to as early as 1913 where, in
Provincia Deserta, Pound was already fracturing the line into
an architecture of rhythmic pauses:

At Rochecoart,
Where the hills part
            in three ways,
And three valleys, full of winding roads,
Fork out to south and north
There is a place of trees . . . grey with lichen.

13   Routledge and Kegan Paul, London, 1964.

That is Pound in 1913. Here is Williams thirty years later in
the poem that came to be called *The Descent*, building on
discoveries Pound had made available earlier in the century:

>   The descent beckons
>   as the ascent beckoned.
>   Memory is a kind
>   of accomplishment,
>   a sort of renewal
>   even
>   an initiation.

Now W. C. Williams, like his friend Pound, had learned
much that he could convert to poetic usage from the Vorticist
group in which Pound was active. Although Williams was not
in London at the time, he read the Vorticist periodical *Blast*.
In the second issue, the sculptor Gaudier Brzeska wrote a
manifesto in which he spoke of deriving his emotions as
sculptor from the arrangement of surfaces, from the lines and
planes defining surfaces. In a fascinating unpublished essay
of 1915 called 'Vortex – W. C. W.' Williams translates the
terms of Gaudier's manifesto into the terms of a poetry where
the word 'plane' is used to reinforce Williams' idea of a poetry
of line pulling against line, a poetry where the sense of
physical resistance is paramount, where words and groups of
words make up the resistant facets of a poem – a terminology
obviously opposed to the impressionistic drift of contemporary free verse in writers like Amy Lowell.

By 1913, Pound, in fragmenting the line into rhythmic
components, was beginning that shift of emphasis to the
weight and duration of each syllable, what Davie speaks of as
'the reconstituting of the verse line as the poetic unit, slowing
down the surge from one line into the next in such a way that
smaller components within the line (down to the very
syllables) can recover weight and value'.

When, in 1913, Mrs Fenollosa sent Pound her husband's
notes, what time and again must have sprung to Pound's
attention was the way Chinese poetry is a poetry where the
line unit is the unit of attention – line on line, with clear
components but seldom enjambing with the next line. So

translation in *Cathay* became for Pound an exploration into the possibilities of extending his *own* poetry: he was not just doing a job (like the Penguin translator of Sophocles' *Theban Plays*); he was growing as a poet, he was extending that emotional concentration he was already seeking for in heaving against the Edwardian idiom, against the fluent slackness of much then-contemporary verse.

Pound had, in fact, begun this redirection before Mary Fenollosa sent him her husband's notebooks. He had begun it with Oriental models in mind. Like Fenollosa, he came to Chinese via Japanese. What had initially interested him was the compactness of Japanese haiku – those little three line poems. Already by 1913, he had condensed (after six months' work) a much longer poem into the haiku-like brevity of the famous *In a Station of the Metro*:

> The apparition   of these faces   in the crowd:
> Petals   on a wet, black bough.

He had noted there the way in haiku the insight often presents itself as an isolated image, not just a simile introduced by the word 'like', but by the paratactic alignment with the initial experience of the poem: one thing held over against another, divided and yet united by the electric spark which flies between them.

This basic insight is what distinguishes Pound's orientalizing from that of sinologists like H. A. Giles or from a lot of Arthur Waley: it is what allies the man and the moment. As I have pointed out earlier, the moment of Pound's *Cathay* was the moment of the Vorticist movement, the moment when, in England, the machine, cubism and (among other things) the Japanese print had produced unexpected consequences. Japan was in the air from Gilbert and Sullivan's *Mikado* of 1884 to Puccini's *Madame Butterfly* of 1904, from the *japonerie* of Whistler's paintings to the prints painted in the background of a dozen Van Goghs. The Japanese, in fact, were also opening themselves to the west: hence Fenollosa's presence in Tokyo, an American from Harvard who went as Professor of Philosophy in 1878 and stayed on to become

Imperial Commissioner of Fine Arts. Pound, speaking of the new insights he had gained via Vorticist art in *The Egoist* in June 1914, wrote:

> I trust the gentle reader is accustomed to take pleasure in 'Whistler and the Japanese'.
>
> From Whistler and the Japanese, or Chinese, the 'world', that is to say, the fragment of the English-speaking world which spreads itself in print, learned to enjoy 'arrangements' of colours and masses.

So much for Pound.

Europe's greatest debt to the Japanese print – cheap, and long collected by artists – was this lesson of formal disposition, this tendency to abstract forms, the arrangement (as Pound says) of colours and masses. One sees why Pound should have considered himself a Vorticist, for there is surely a parallel between Pound's poetry, drawing attention to its own linearity, and to its segmenting of that linearity into lengths meant to be *clearly heard,* and a visual art of colours and masses in arrangement, reacting (like Pound) against vagueness, and using sharp line, facet and plane meant to be *clearly seen* and not dissolved away into *sfumato,* into the mists and twilights of *symbolisme.* 'These new men', says Pound in his book on Gaudier,

> have made me see form, have made me more conscious of the appearance of the sky where it juts down between houses, of the bright pattern of sunlight which the bath water throws upon the ceiling, of the great 'V's' of light that dart through the chinks over the curtain rings, all these are new chords, new keys of design.

Vorticism itself, having learned from the very faceted, very planar art of Cézanne, was (like early cubism) a movement of translation – translation from Oriental art and from so-called primitive art. Somewhat like Pound in *Cathay,* the artists translated 'without knowing the language' – they wanted the simplified, dynamic forms for their own purposes, regardless of the *tribal* meanings or functions of (say) African fetishes. The pre-war years, in London and Paris, were, like the Renaissance, one of the great phases of cultural translation, of metamorphosis in the widest sense. The artists of the

Renaissance wanted to live with the forms of classical antiquity. The artists of 1912 wanted to live with the forms of China, Japan, Africa and the South Sea Islands. As Gaudier Brzeska headily writes in *Blast* for June 1914:

> The knowledge of our civilisation embraces the world [. . .] We have been influenced by what we liked most, each according to his own individuality, we have crystallised the sphere into the cube, we have made a combination of all the possible shaped masses.

Anyone who visited the Vorticist show in London in the spring and summer of 1974 at the Hayward Gallery must have realized that, as Pound saw it, London *was*, for a phase, a vortex, drawing energies into itself, and re-using them − hence Pound's label for the movement. A vortex for Pound meant a cone of energy, a whirling force attracting outside energies to itself. London, thought Pound, could be another Rome, 'a vortex drawing strength from the peripheries'. Wyndham Lewis wrote: 'We will convert the king if possible. A VORTICIST KING! WHY NOT?' Here in London existed the most far-reaching single art movement that, with the exception of pre-Raphaelitism, Britain has ever known, but it was to be tragically foreshortened by the war. Its members were scattered. Gaudier was killed, Lewis went away to the front and his principal Vorticist canvases − fifteen or more very large paintings − were lost or destroyed. No London dealer took up the Vorticists as Vollard and Kahnweiler took up the cubists in Paris. By the 1920s the movement was forgotten and the Bloomsbury set, in the shape of Roger Fry and Clive Bell, prevailed as arbiters of taste. In 1937 Lewis characterized himself and his contemporaries as 'the men of 1914', 'the men of a Future that has not materialised'.

The wave of energy throughout Europe and England, which made men like Pound believe they were living in a new Renaissance, was spent in England by the First World War. It had its renewals in Paris. It reached Russia (until group antagonisms and political suppression ended it there) in the work of Malevitch, Popova, Kliun, Tatlin and the constructivists: El Lissitsky, another masterly artist, was inspired by the typography and illustrations of Lewis' magazine, *Blast*. The Revolution extended for a while in Russia what the war and Bloomsbury sapped in England. Gaudier dead; Lewis impoverished; forgotten as a painter, since, for ten years, from 1921 onwards, he never exhibited; Pound demoralized and, like D. H. Lawrence, abandoning the England on which he had centred his hopes for a new age; Pound in Italy swallowing Mussolini whole. These were the sad facts of the twenties.

Cathay already had preluded a tragic atmosphere beyond and above the exciting rhetoric of the Vorticist manifestos. The man was a great translator. The moment was of an era of cultural translation – from Japanese, Chinese and from Easter Island forms. It was also the moment of the assassination of the Austrian archduke at Sarajevo. These *Cathay* poems of departures and battles were being worked on in 1914, the first year of the war. When Gaudier received the book in 1915 he was in the trenches. He wrote back to Mrs Shakespear:

> I use [the book] to put courage into my fellows. I speak now of the 'Bowmen' and [. . . 'Lament of the Frontier Guard'] which are so appropriate to our case.
> (Ezra Pound, *Gaudier Brzeska* (New Directions, 1970)
> p. 68)

Pound admired the implicitness of Chinese poetry – as he shows in his note to *The Jewel Stairs* – and there is an implicit relation between these translations and the war itself. Hugh Kenner in his book *The Pound Era* (p. 202) has brilliantly pointed out the way in which this admiration of implicitness is made over into the implicitness of the translation. Kenner praises *Cathay* for bringing the past abreast of the present – the present being the First World War:

> *Cathay* is largely a war-book using Fenollosa's [cribs] much as Pope used Horace or Johnson Juvenal, to supply a system of parallels and a structure of discourse [. . .] Perfectly vital after half a century, they are among the most durable of all poetic responses to World War I.

Kenner's apposite and moving sentences celebrate a moment when poems from a remote age were suddenly metamor-

phosed into poems of present consequence, when the recoverable past renewed itself at a time of tragedy and of European
chaos. It is an old story – and takes us back by way of
epilogue to one of Pound's acknowledged forebears, also the
witness of a disordered time – Gavin Douglas and his Virgil.
Greater than the original, according to Pound. Certainly a
translation capturing, as none other does, that sense of
instability and threat to civilized values that gives an
undertow to Virgil's cadences. Again, it is a story of the man
and the moment – a time of imminent disorders and daily
insecurities culminating in the battle of Flodden in 1513 and
the destruction of Scotland's youth. It was in that very year,
1513, that Douglas completed his *Aeneid* – a year whose train
of disasters involved not only the spirit of that undertaking,
but his ultimate exile and death. The story is too long to be
told here, but once again it is one where the tensions and
energies of an age found expression in an effort of poetic
recovery – a literary metempsychosis of Virgil in Renaissance
Scotland – and where a translation stood in the forefront of
the creative works of its era, much as Pound's *Cathay* to the
twentieth century, and Dryden's major translations and
Pope's to their respective ages.